Damien Hirst, Beautiful Primal Urges Rug, 2014

TORY BURCH
IN COLOR

FOREWORD BY ANNA WINTOUR

EDITED BY NANDINI D'SOUZA WOLFE

Abrams, New York

For my children, my brothers and my parents, Buddy and Reva

CONTENTS

FOREWORD

BY ANNA WINTOUR

Tory first entered *Vogue*'s orbit 15 years ago, a very stylish young Manhattan mother about town with a strong, personal take on all-American style.

We very soon discovered, however, that she is far more than a beautiful, culturally aware New Yorker—she's also an influential tastemaker, and a brilliant businesswoman who has since applied her taste and serious work ethic to building and sustaining a billion-dollar brand.

Tory has always been family-oriented. Early on, we celebrated the dynamic interiors that she'd put together in Southampton and on Fifth Avenue—homes that were brilliantly colored, formal yet quirky and filled with treasures—and I remember being struck by how essentially child-friendly they were. I've always loved the image of Tory's youngest son, Sawyer, on his tricycle in the family's cavernous marble entrance hall in their apartment at the Pierre Hotel, and the one of her twin boys, Nick and Henry, playing with their bows and arrows on the silk velvet sofa in their living room.

At the start, very few people knew that as Tory was juggling the demands of motherhood—with an extended family of six children!—she was also hatching a very focused plan to launch her eponymous fashion line.

From the very beginning, Tory had a powerful vision for her brand, with a signature as emphatic and appealing as that of a modern-day Lilly Pulitzer. Rooted in the hip, Sixties style of her beloved parents, her vibrant aesthetic soon crossed effortlessly from fashion and accessories into different fields, including home and fragrance. It was an immediate success—Tory sold 300,000 pairs of those buckled ballet slippers (named for her mother, Reva, naturally) in the first year alone.

And why not? Who wouldn't want to be Tory Burch? She's admirable in so many ways. She is charming and she's humble, she's a fantastic mother and a devoted friend, and she's proved herself to be, quite simply, a truly sensational businesswoman.

Tory has an innate sense of decorum, but that doesn't mean she isn't the life of the party. This is a woman whose cool exterior hides a wicked sense of humor and a great sense of fun. And don't let her polite manner fool you—when Tory sets out to do something, she is not only fiercely determined and completely hands-on, she thoroughly engages with every detail. And while she may be low-key about her philanthropy, its reach is incredibly impactful. Through the Tory Burch Foundation, she empowers American women with small loans, mentorship and entrepreneurial education.

There's no doubt that Tory is a true role model for our time. But perhaps what I admire most about her is the way she keeps a sense of balance. She enjoys being a mother, she enjoys her success and all that comes with it, but above all, she keeps life in perspective. And that's a talent that any of us can appreciate.

INTRODUCTION

I SEE THE WORLD IN COLOR. It's the first thing I notice. I am drawn to the way colors
interact with and complement one another… The subtle variations within the same shade:
navy, cornflower and periwinkle or orange, mandarin and coral. Living in full color is my
guiding principle—from the way I raise my children to the way I approach my work.

"Huck Finn meets Andy Warhol" is how my brother Jamie describes our Kodachrome
childhood. My parents, Buddy and Reva Robinson, raised my brothers Robert, Jamie, Leonard
and me on a farm in Valley Forge, at the end of the Main Line in Pennsylvania. They taught
us to embrace differences in people and ideas and to surround ourselves with beauty and
imagination. Even our family dinners every night were as special as they were with guests—
table linens, tureens and flowers. On any given day, there was always a wide spectrum of people
at our home: sculptors, interior designers, artists, poets, actors, musicians, first (and second)
cousins and a slew of school friends. My parents were adventurers who took six-week journeys

to Greece, Italy, Morocco and India. On these trips they collected lifelong friends and beautiful things. Their enthusiasm and wanderlust rubbed off on all of us.

When I was an art history major at the University of Pennsylvania, my sense of color was refined by studying Henri Matisse, Gustav Klimt, Ellsworth Kelly and Josef Albers. When I started working in fashion, I learned from an incredible group of designers and business leaders: Zoran, Ralph Lauren, Vera Wang, Narciso Rodriguez and, of course, the team at Tory Burch—each colorful in his or her unique way.

This book is a kaleidoscope of those influences and experiences, told through images and stories of the people, places, things and ideas that inspire me. While 256 pages (an auspicious number that our company feng shui master, Mr. Yung Siu, suggested) isn't enough to cover all the shades and combinations I love, the following 11 colors represent the ones that mean the most to me.

All the best,

Tory

Marrakech, 2013

O range has been my favorite color for as long as I can remember. When I was five, I wanted to paint my bedroom mandarin or coral, but my mother thought it was a little too much. We went with Kelly green. Decades later, my wish came true when we opened our first boutique, on Elizabeth Street, and the doors were bright orange lacquer. I love orange; it's happy and chic. It comes in so many shades, from poppy to melon, and they all cast a warm glow. It is an unexpected choice in fashion and at home, which is why I like it. Orange reminds me of David Hicks's graphic interiors and the cover of my favorite album, *Harvest*, by Neil Young. Even though at any given moment my desk is covered with newspapers, sketches, pictures and notes, the glass jar of bright California apricots is hard to miss.

AN IDEA, A COMPANY, A TEAM

We opened our doors at 257 Elizabeth Street in New York City on February 8, 2004. These would be metaphoric doors, of course—the actual orange lacquer ones didn't arrive in time for the opening. On that day, as I was still unpacking boxes—minutes before the first guests arrived—I remember feeling nervous but exhilarated. The idea, in hindsight, sounds almost too simple: design a well-priced collection that my friends and I would want to wear and sell them in a store that feels like a living room.

Just a few years earlier, in 2001, I had been at a crossroads—one of those intersections of the personal and the professional that we all face from time to time. Sawyer, my youngest son, was a baby, and my twins, Nicholas and Henry, were three. I had decided to take

time off after working for 15 years in PR and marketing at Ralph Lauren, Vera Wang and Loewe. While raising the boys, I started thinking about going back to work, but this time, it would be my own business.

Then September 11th happened. The idea of launching a fashion brand felt frivolous. In the months following the tragedy, I found myself watching a lot of CNN, and a commercial about starting a small business kept popping up. Its message, to be brave and follow your dreams, was exactly what I needed to get started.

My initial plan was to revive Jax, an American sportswear brand from the 1960s. My mother wore a lot of Jax, and the clean, sporty lines still felt incredibly modern. I cold-called the owner, Sally Hanson. She passed on the idea, so I started from scratch.

A DAVID HICKS–DESIGNED BEDROOM, ABOVE,
WHICH INSPIRED THE INTERIOR OF THE ELIZABETH STREET BOUTIQUE—OUR FIRST.
PHOTOGRAPHED BY FRANÇOIS HALARD FOR *VOGUE*, 2004.

For inspiration, I didn't have to look further than my parents, Buddy and Reva Robinson. Photos of them traveling and entertaining in the 1960s and '70s fueled my imagination. I started to think about what "lifestyle" meant. This would not be just one category, but a full collection with a boutique and an e-commerce site. With a concept and a business plan, it was time to raise capital. Chris Burch, my ex-husband, and I each invested, and then raised additional funds from over 100 investors.

I began developing the collection with Fiona Kotur Marin, a friend from my days at Ralph Lauren. For two years we worked at my kitchen table with a small group of designers we had put together—Cecile Renna, Suki Wong and Somphone Sikhounmuong, who are still with me today. The team and I did our research. We visited vintage stores and museums and studied old issues of *Vogue* and *Harper's Bazaar* and auction catalogues. Fiona and I brainstormed about things that were hard to find—graphic prints, a colorful tunic, a great tote.

Fiona, who was living in Hong Kong, also introduced us to different manufacturers and to Mona Wu, who would soon become our head of sourcing. If I wasn't in China meeting with factory owners and persuading them to take a chance on us, I was on the phone with Hong Kong.

Advice and insight were critical. People were generous with their time. I asked questions and listened to those who knew more than I did. Tory by TRB was our original brand name. One night at dinner, Kenneth Jay Lane asked me, "Why are you Tory by TRB? It's confusing. Use your own name—you *are* Tory Burch and should be known as that."

I asked my friend Daniel Romualdez, an architect and interior designer, to help design our first boutique. At that time, fashion was in a very minimal place, but I wanted to go in a different direction. Daniel was working with me on my apartment, and the store was meant to be an extension of that. I kept coming back to rooms David Hicks had created—geometric prints and bold colors mixed with pieces from his travels to places like Morocco. For our store, we went with an orange-and-brass motif, inspired by a bedroom and powder room he had designed.

The day we opened, we didn't know what to expect. I asked my family and my friends to come; they asked their friends. By 6 p.m., we had almost sold through our inventory.

IN ELIZABETH STREET, 2006; A WALL OF ORANGE POPPIES DESIGNED BY HELENA LEHANE, IN OUR MADISON AVENUE BOUTIQUE; AND OUR PRESIDENT, BRIGITTE KLEINE.

Word of mouth was, and is, critical for us. About a year later, Adam Glassman from *O* magazine sent one of our tunics to Oprah Winfrey. Her producers called (at first, I thought it was one of my brothers joking with me) and invited me to be on the show. Her team warned us to prepare toryburch.com and our boutique for heavy traffic. The following week, we had 8 million hits on our site!

We quickly realized there was demand, and we had to figure out how to sustain and grow. Finding the right people was key. We needed a president. I met Brigitte Kleine. She had great experience, having worked at Donna Karan, Michael Kors and Alexander McQueen. Our first meeting was in my apartment. The chaos of a start-up and my boys running around didn't faze her. Brigitte has been an incredible partner who shares my vision and ambition to create a different kind of company. After much persistence, I convinced my brother Robert Isen to join as President of Corporate Development and Chief Legal Officer. The team grew, and together we have scaled beyond our original five-store business plan (we are at 120) and navigated the sometimes-choppy waters of recessions and the complexities of international expansion.

Our focus has always been on how we connect with our customers. When we launched, social media was a new phenomenon. For a young brand with no marketing budget, it was a powerful way to connect. But we wanted to do it differently. We brought together a group of magazine editors, led by our Creative Director Honor Brodie, to create our blog and Tory Daily app. We embraced content and infused our website and social channels with an editorial point of view. Through a blog post, a tweet or an Instagram photo, we have been able to tell our stories and those of emerging brands, artists, musicians and entrepreneurs.

When I started the company, one of my goals was to one day be able to establish a foundation. Entrepreneurs inspired us to create the Tory Burch Foundation, which supports the economic empowerment of women through small business loans, mentorship and entrepreneurial education. The work of the foundation has become a core part of the entire company's mission.

Through it all, our company culture guides us. It is inspired by the way my parents raised me—to be kind, to always treat others with respect and to strive for excellence. Even though it has been 10 years, it feels like we are just beginning.

Athens, 1970s

"I NEVER THOUGHT
I'D BE FAMOUS FOR A SHOE!"

—REVA ROBINSON

THE STORY OF THE REVA

The Reva ballerina. Its success took us by surprise when we introduced it in 2006. Then again, it's named after my mother— the most stylish woman I know. It combines two of my favorite concepts: the effortless chic of a ballet flat and the graphic feel of our logo. From the moment I started working on the company, I knew that a logo would be important. I wanted one that was different; I wanted it to be a unique design, something beautiful and bold that people would want to wear. The double-T logo draws inspiration from Moroccan architecture and David Hicks's interiors. We worked on so many options, but only one stood out. I knew it as soon as I saw it. It was emotional. I always find it interesting to hear people's reactions to it in China, our team has heard from customers that the logo looks like an artist's seal and that the gold is auspicious.

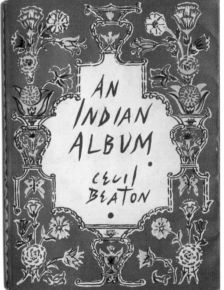

THE LIBRARY

In New York, we live in this room. It's where we read, watch movies, play Scrabble, hang out. It's a happy, cozy room, and great for entertaining. The design team and I watch inspiration movies here, and company brainstorming meetings have taken place around the coffee table. People feel they can come in and put their feet up. I love that. The bookshelves are lined with my favorite books and objects: baskets from Haiti, armor from Japan, my collection of porcelain stirrup cups and, of course, pictures of family and friends. This room looks out over Central Park. In the fall, it's spectacular with extraordinary colors—we designed the room after the leaves.

RIGHT: A MARK ROTHKO
PAINTING HANGS
IN A BILLY BALDWIN–
DESIGNED APARTMENT
IN NEW YORK. TWO
PEOPLE I'VE ALWAYS
ADMIRED. BALDWIN'S
PHILOSOPHY WAS
DOWN-TO-EARTH:
"BE FAITHFUL TO
YOUR OWN TASTE
BECAUSE NOTHING
YOU REALLY LIKE
IS EVER OUT OF STYLE."

Mark Rothko, Orange and Red on Red, 1957

I've always been drawn to Rothko's bold, wide bands of tonal color.

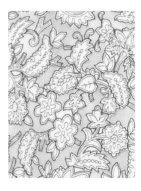

ROMY SCHNEIDER'S
CÔTE D'AZUR LOOK IN
1969'S *LA PISCINE*
INFLUENCED SPRING
2014. ORANGE IS
BRIGHT AND CAN BE
A BIT EXTREME, WHICH
IS WHY I LIKE IT. IT
COMES IN SO MANY
SHADES, IT LOOKS
GOOD ON EVERYONE,
LIKE CORAL THAT
HAS A PINK CAST,
RIGHT, ON THE RUNWAY,
OR FAR LEFT, ON
CAMILA ALVES, WITH
BROOKLYN DECKER.

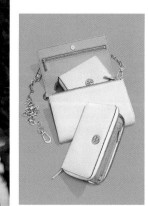

A COLORFUL YET
SERENE DAY ON
A DESIGN TRIP
THROUGH FORTE
DEI MARMI,
ITALY, IN 2011.

THE SCREWDRIVER

INGREDIENTS
3 oz vodka
5 oz blood-orange juice
2 oz club soda
Ice
Blood-orange wedges

DIRECTIONS
Pour vodka, blood-orange juice,
club soda and ice into a glass and top off
with a blood-orange wedge.

Nick & Henry, Southampton, 2000

MY IDENTICAL TWINS

Henry and Nicholas don't know who's older.
I'll tell them when they're 21. Not telling
them was one of the best decisions I have
ever made, it takes competition out of the
equation. They are best friends with each
other and their little brother, and people
can't tell them apart.

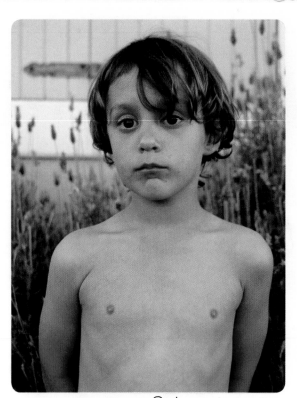

Bahamas, 2007

THE YOUNGEST ONE

Sawyer is about seven years old here;
we were in the Bahamas. Giant starfish
were everywhere, and we stayed in
the water for hours. I think this was the
start of his fishing career. He has since
become an avid fisherman.

THE FOUNDATION

One of the reasons I wanted to start a business was to create a foundation for women and children. The idea wasn't well received at the time. People told me never to use the word "foundation" or "social responsibility" when talking to potential investors. But giving back was always part of the plan and has become a part of the company's DNA. We have learned that the Tory Burch Foundation, which we launched in 2009 to empower women entrepreneurs through business loans, entrepreneurial education and mentoring, is as important to us as a company and to our customers as it is to the women we support.

The fact is, women think differently. Based on our experiences, we see the world through our particular lens and, in turn, do things in a unique way. (To my three brothers and three sons: not better, just differently.) There has been a positive shift toward companies' and countries' recognizing that women are the key to economic growth around the world. We are grateful to and inspired by our partners— Goldman Sachs's 10,000 Women and Bank of America—who share our commitment to women entrepreneurs and are dedicated to making a difference. There is still a lot of work to be done. This is one small step: 100% of the gross proceeds we receive from the sale of this book will benefit the Tory Burch Foundation.

Ipanema Beach, 2012

"A great sapphire it was whose light and cradle
Held all things: there were the delights of skies, though
Its cloudness blue was different; of sea and meadow,
But their shapes not seen…."

—W.S. MERWIN

Blue—I wear navy like most people
wear black. For our first few seasons, the collection's darkest color was midnight. Blue against black,
cornflower with green, navy-and-blush. For as long as I can remember, my parents have
collected blue-and-white export china; I started collecting it, too. Ginger jars and spongeware jugs filled
with blue hydrangeas from our garden; International Klein Blue, made famous by Yves Klein, one of
my favorite artists; and blue-and-white striped sailor shirts—which never go out of style.

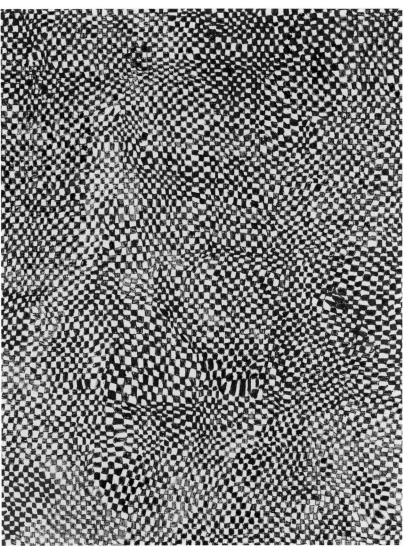

Harmony Korine, Blue Checker, 2014

THE CLASH: MEXICAN
CLAY PLATES, TURKISH
TABLE LINENS, ITALIAN
RESIN TUMBLERS, AMERICAN
SPONGEWARE JUGS
(WITH PEONIES FROM
THE GARDEN)–LUNCH AT
HOME IN SOUTHAMPTON.

THE KITCHEN TABLE

The key to our company's success is the
people. Several of the women pictured here,
for *Elle*, are part of the original team
who sat at my kitchen table in 2003 and 2004.
They are, from left to right, Cecile Rena,
Suki Wong, Maggie Ragucci, Gigi Mortimer,
Linda Waddington-McEwan, Stephanie von
Watzdorf and Somphone Sikhounmuong.

The room has become affectionately
known as the Blue Room. I kept coming back
to this signature Billy Baldwin cotton-fabric
wall covering that was inspired by Matisse,
my favorite artist.

Topkapi Palace, Istanbul, 2013

PATTERN ON PATTERN

Ever since I first walked through the Topkapi
Palace in Istanbul, I have been fascinated
with Iznik tilework. Pookie, my stepdaughter,
found Iksel, a Paris-based company that
makes paper wall panels of hand-painted tiles.
We spent days piecing together our own
layout for our dining room in Southampton,
right, photographed by Norman Jean Roy.

I LIKE BIG BUNCHES OF
FLOWERS, LIKE THESE BLUE
AND PURPLE DELPHINIUMS
AND PEEGEE HYDRANGEAS,
IN CHINESE EXPORT GINGER
JARS AND SPONGEWARE
JUGS. SOME OF THE FLOWERS
COME FROM OUR GARDEN,
OTHERS FROM THE CHELSEA
FLOWER MARKET.

RAÚL ÀVILA ON
PERFECT FLOWERS

The event and floral designer's advice…

Vase you like best…
Always pottery, often blue and white.
It's nice when the vase blends
with the color of the flowers.

How do you prep for a party at home?
Put flowers in the foyer—they're the
first thing your guests see. And
then small arrangements in the living
and dining rooms.

Best flower to give a woman…
Peonies.

…and a man?
Green-and-white parrot tulips.

THE TUNIC

I found this green floral tunic in
a Paris flea market. It was the
first silhouette in our collection and
is a quintessential wardrobe staple,
epitomizing a chic, effortless attitude of
women in the Seventies, including
my mother. Après-swim, she would tie
up her wet hair and throw on a
caftan—unbelievably stylish.

THE TUNIC—THE ULTIMATE
IN BOHEMIAN GLAMOUR.
CLOCKWISE FROM
TOP LEFT: SPRING 2013;
MOROCCAN LANTERNS;
GRACE KELLY, 1954;
JEAN SHRIMPTON, 1970;
PRINCE, IN THE SAME
TUNIC I'M WEARING
ON THE PREVIOUS PAGE;
ALI MACGRAW, 1970;
SPRING 2014; KENNETH
JAY LANE AT HOME, 1964.

GLOBAL ARTISTS

I have loved tie-dye since high school.
It reminds me of my first concert and endless
summers. Many cultures, like those in
India, Japan and Africa, have a tradition
of dyeing that is unique to their region.
The tie-dye pieces from our Spring 2013
runway were handmade by women artisans
in the Republic of Guinea, through a
partnership with the nonprofit organization
There Is No Limit Foundation. These artists
are keeping traditions alive, while
supporting their families and communities.

I AM SUPERSTITIOUS. I KNOCK ON WOOD, CARRY A RED RIBBON FOR GOOD LUCK AND LOVE EVIL EYES.
I WAS TOLD THEY WOULD ALWAYS KEEP ME AND EVERYONE I LOVE SAFE.

Texture, tapestry, brocades & florals

FALL 2014

This collection was inspired by armor.
I was surrounded with it when growing up.
My grandfather and parents collected it.
I remember going through the house being
a little scared by all of the swords, shields and
suits. Now, I love the oversized proportions
and the mix of textures and patterns. We
translated the lines of this suit of armor,
right, into a sweater for Fall.

Richard Diebenkorn, Ocean Park No. 68, 1974

CLEAN LINES—OUR PERRY GUILLOT-DESIGNED POOL.

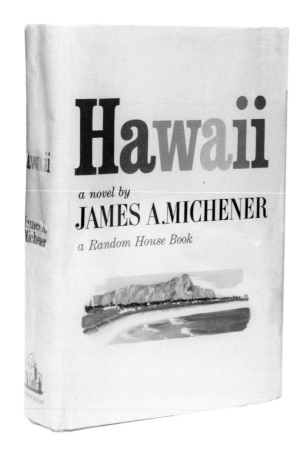

BEST BEACH READS

Sitting by the water is the best place to catch up on my reading list. Holding an actual book in my hands, uninterrupted for an hour, is a luxury. My mother gave me her copy of James A. Michener's 1959 novel, *Hawaii*, which has made the rounds in our family. We are constantly giving each other books. Here are some of our favorites:

One Hundred Years of Solitude
Gabriel García Márquez

The House of Mirth
Edith Wharton

The Thorn Birds
Colleen McCullough

Pride and Prejudice
Jane Austen

The French Lieutenant's Woman
John Fowles

Tender Is the Night
F. Scott Fitzgerald

My favorite poem

ITHAKA

As you set out for Ithaka
hope the voyage is a long one,
full of adventure, full of discovery.
Laistrygonians and Cyclops,
angry Poseidon—don't be afraid of them:
you'll never find things like that on your way
as long as you keep your thoughts raised high,
as long as a rare excitement
stirs your spirit and your body.
Laistrygonians and Cyclops,
wild Poseidon—you won't encounter them
unless you bring them along inside your soul,
unless your soul sets them up in front of you.

Hope the voyage is a long one.
May there be many a summer morning when,
with what pleasure, what joy,
you come into harbors seen for the first time;
may you stop at Phoenician trading stations
to buy fine things,
mother of pearl and coral, amber and ebony,
sensual perfume of every kind—
as many sensual perfumes as you can;
and may you visit many Egyptian cities
to gather stores of knowledge from their scholars.

Keep Ithaka always in your mind.
Arriving there is what you are destined for.
But do not hurry the journey at all.
Better if it lasts for years,
so you are old by the time you reach the island,
wealthy with all you have gained on the way,
not expecting Ithaka to make you rich.

Ithaka gave you the marvelous journey.
Without her you would not have set out.
She has nothing left to give you now.

And if you find her poor, Ithaka won't have fooled you.
Wise as you will have become, so full of experience,
you will have understood by then what these Ithakas mean.

—C. P. CAVAFY

THE COLOSSUS

OF MAROUSSI   HENRY
MILLER

A BOOK ABOUT GREECE BY THE AUTHOR OF TROPIC OF CANCER

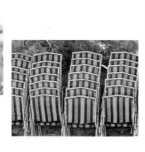

LIYA KEBEDE ON
HER PHILOSOPHY & STYLE

The mother, model and Founder of lemlem—a collection designed by
(and that benefits) artisans in her native Ethiopia.

Lessons you've learned from lemlem…

That you don't have to have all the answers at the
beginning. Sometimes the most important part
is just starting.

And from the artisans who design the collection…

Working alongside people who conceptualize, design and
handcraft lemlem has given me a greater appreciation
for the scale of both the work and the love that go into
a collection. Every piece is different, reinforcing for me
the need to preserve originality in the fashion industry.

What do you hope to teach your children?

I love traveling with them and opening their eyes to other
cultures. Ultimately, I hope that they will cherish family,
health, freedom, respect and creativity as much as I do.

What's your life philosophy?

We all have the power to create change. If you have an
idea, see it through, no matter how silly or daunting.

What's your favorite color?

I don't have a favorite—I like them all.

Southampton, 2013

"The Owl and the Pussy-Cat went to sea
In a beautiful pea-green boat."

—EDWARD LEAR

Green is so many things—Adirondack,
Kelly, army, or that perfect lettuce green in Dodie Thayer's pottery. In 2009, my boys and I hiked
up to the summit of Machu Picchu, in Peru. It was breathtaking. The view was vast, all shades of green.
Green is tomboy in olives, glamorous as Indochine's palm leaf wallpaper, delicate as the Queen Anne's lace
from my garden. And of all the colors, it's the one I most associate with scent. It reminds me of early mornings,
smelling fresh-cut grass out of my childhood bedroom window. Or of vetiver, which my father always wore.

"WITHOUT AN
INTERESTING INTERIOR,
I CAN'T MAKE AN
INTERESTING PICTURE."
–TINA BARNEY

A TINA BARNEY PORTRAIT

This was a fantastic day. Tina Barney
photographed a fictional family (we cast
Madison Malerba, Trish Goff, Polly
Mellen and Noot Seear) wearing our Spring
2010 collection in my apartment. There's
an intimacy to her photographs, like you're
looking through a window at a particular
moment in time in a particular family's life.
And interiors are always another character
in Tina's images. "People's clothes sort of
match their interiors," she told me on
set. "And they're not always aware of that."
When I was designing this collection,
I was actually working on my living room…

FROM LEFT: A BILLY
BALDWIN—DESIGNED
SITTING ROOM
WITH VELVET WALLS;
HUBERT DE GIVENCHY
IN HIS LIVING ROOM
(HIS VELVET COUCH
INSPIRED MINE);
AND YVES SAINT
LAURENT'S SALON
IN HIS PARIS
COUTURE HOUSE.

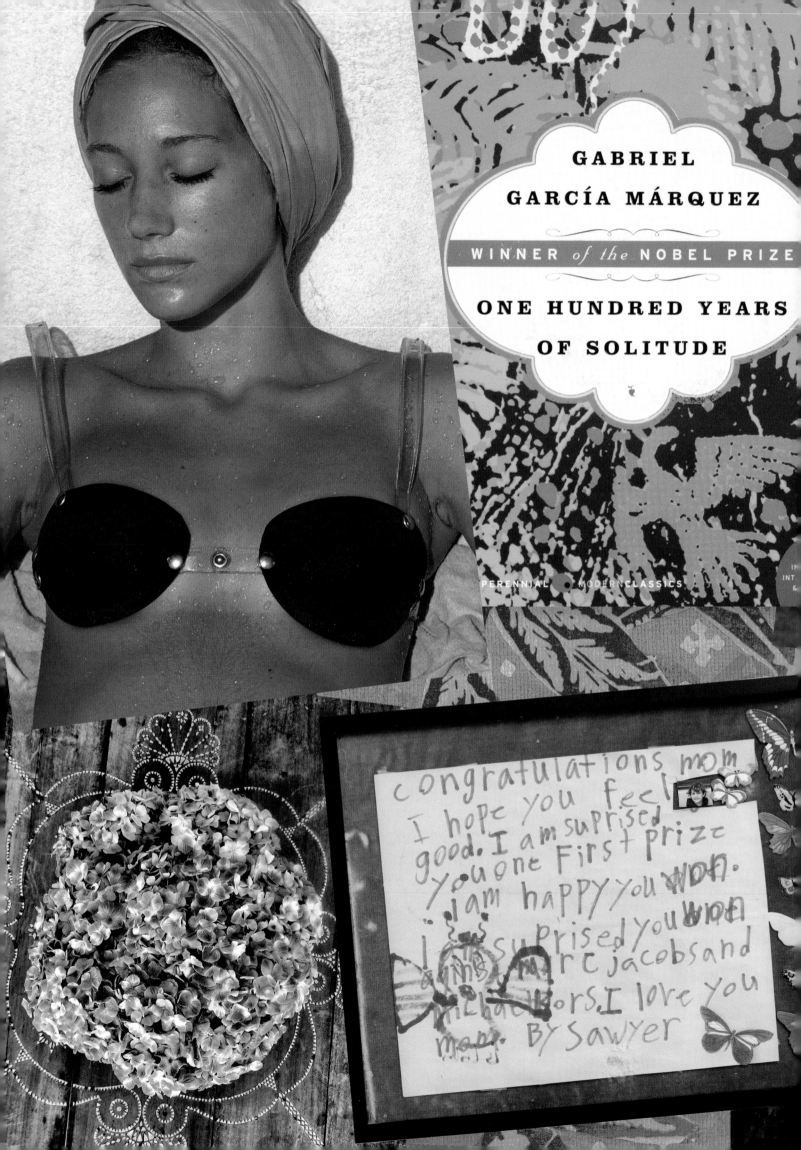

CLOCKWISE FROM TOP LEFT, MARISA BERENSON IN CAPRI, 1968; MY FAVORITE BOOK OF ALL TIME; HANNELI MUSTAPARTA MIXING FLORALS AND OUR SPRING 2013 BAG; A SHELL PLANTER I FOUND AT LES PUCES FLEA MARKET IN PARIS; A BOOK I LOVE TO GIVE (AND REREAD MYSELF); FLOWERS IN SOUTHAMPTON; A CONGRATULATIONS NOTE FROM SAWYER WHEN I WON THE CFDA FOR ACCESSORIES IN 2007; AND HYDRANGEAS FROM MY GARDEN.

THE MADELEINE CASTAING INFLUENCE

Madeleine Castaing is a *decorator's decorator*, influencing generations of designers from David Hicks to Jacques Grange. In every room, she exercised her full imagination, using a powerful blue-and-black combination in one apartment, mixing furniture from different countries and eras in another.

There's a controlled abandon to her designs that I love. Castaing's blue-and-green Rayure Fleurie fabric in a powder room in Southampton, opposite, and a room designed by Grange, above. Castaing's ideas and colorways also inspired rooms in our Madison Avenue and Rodeo Drive boutiques.

GREEN HAS A SENSE OF NOSTALGIA FOR MY FRIEND TABITHA SIMMONS,
A DESIGNER AND OUR RUNWAY STYLIST (WEARING FALL 2013):
"I ASSOCIATE IT WITH HAPPINESS AND THE ENGLISH COUNTRYSIDE,
WHERE I WAS BORN." SHE'S PARTIAL TO OLIVE AND MILITARY HUES:
"NOTHING BEATS A GREAT MILITARY PARKA WORN WITH A CHIFFON DRESS."

Scarabs—an Art Nouveau motif & favorite design detail

Dodie, Palm Beach, 1970s

DODIE THAYER

Dodie Thayer is a true American artisan.
Her story is remarkable: Her ancestors
helped settle Palm Beach, Florida, where
she taught herself how to cast pottery
from lettuce and cabbage leaves, creating
a range of tureens, plates and *objets*
through trial and error.

Jacqueline Kennedy Onassis and C. Z.
Guest collected her signature lettuce ware.
I love how the fresh green looks against
eggshell blue. In 2013, I reached out to Dodie
and asked if she would be interested in
collaborating with us. She said yes! And we
are working on our first collection together,
Dodie Thayer for Tory Burch, for 2015.

When we visited her at home on the
Loxahatchee River in Jupiter, Florida, we
talked about how her designs struck
such a chord. "They are big and showy,"
she said. And did she have any advice
for entrepreneurs? "Try different things.
Be self-reliant."

Ellsworth Kelly, Wild Grape, 1961

"MY AIM IS TO CAPTURE
THE LIGHT AND ENERGY OF COLOR."

—ELLSWORTH KELLY

Racquet back! Racquet back!

MY FAMILY SPENT LONG
HOURS ON OUR TENNIS
COURT. MY MOM WOULD
ALWAYS SAY "SIDE TO THE
NET! EYE ON THE BALL!"
IT WAS OUR FAMILY TIME,
PLAYING ROUND-ROBINS
WELL PAST MIDNIGHT.
THERE WAS AN ENORMOUS
TREE NEXT TO THE COURT
THAT WE WOULD CLIMB
FOR A BIRD'S-EYE VIEW.

THE ORIGINAL POOL
HOUSE IN SOUTHAMPTON
HAD GREAT BONES.
WE REPAINTED, REFURBISHED
AND ADDED LIGHT-PINK
GARDEN ROSES. IT
TOOK TWO YEARS FOR
THE ROSES TO CLIMB
ALL THE WAY TO THE TOP
OF THE LATTICE.

THE SOUTHSIDE

INGREDIENTS
1½ oz vodka

½ oz Cointreau

1 oz simple syrup

2½ oz fresh lime juice

Ice

Soda water

Fresh mint leaves

DIRECTIONS
Muddle mint leaves in a pitcher.
Add vodka, Cointreau, simple syrup,
lime juice and ice. Stir well.
Top off with soda water (but don't stir).
Add mint sprig.

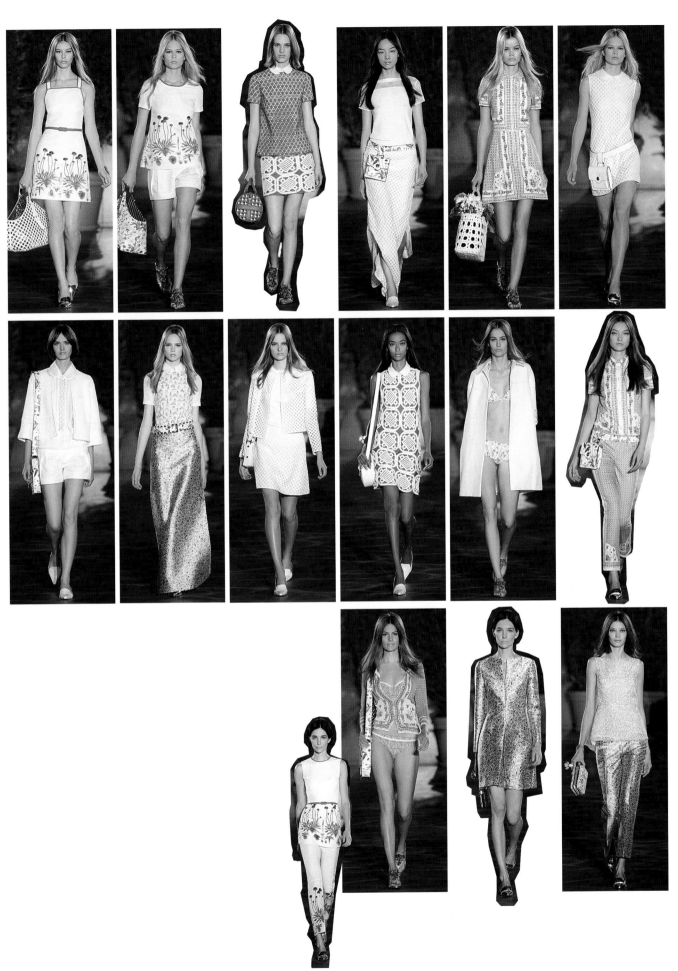

SPRING 2014—BOTANICALS,
ARCHITECTURE AND CLEAN SIXTIES
SILHOUETTES. TRELLISES INSPIRED OUR
TEXTURES. A PICTURE I TOOK OF QUEEN
ANNE'S LACE IN MY GARDEN TURNED
INTO DIGITAL AND WATERCOLOR PRINTS.
THE TIGHT BUNCHES OF FLOWERS
REMIND ME OF POINT DE GAZE LACE.

The summit of Machu Picchu with my boys—
one of those moments that stay with you
for the rest of your life.

GUACAMOLE

INGREDIENTS

5 very ripe avocados

3 limes

2 tablespoons white vinegar

5 cilantro branches (chopped)

2 tomatoes (finely chopped)

¼ cup diced red onion

1 or 2 jalapeño peppers (chopped)

½ teaspoon hot sauce

¾ teaspoon sea salt

Salt & Pepper

DIRECTIONS

Mash avocados in a large bowl. Squeeze juice from the limes and add vinegar,
cilantro, tomatoes, onion, jalapeños (use 1 pepper for less spice), hot sauce
and sea salt. Mix well. Add salt and pepper to taste, and a few cilantro leaves.

Henry, Southampton, 2000

Tulum, 2010

"Where ships of purple gently toss
On seas of daffodil,
Fantastic sailors mingle,
And then—the wharf is still."

—EMILY DICKINSON

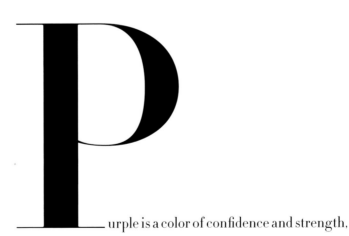

Purple is a color of confidence and strength, often associated with a woman I've always been fascinated by—Cleopatra. I like purple in its pink lilac hues or dark, like eggplant. We often use it when designing: lavender with oatmeal, plum with cornflower blue, or violet with navy. My garden is full of purple, from salvia and delphiniums to pansies and violets. I once went to a home outside of Paris, where I saw the most extraordinary garden—a football-sized field of perfectly manicured lavender. Simple and magnificent. Purple doesn't occur as often as other colors in nature, says feng shui master Mr. Siu. So when it does, it's a good omen.

GARDENS—A BALANCE
OF SCIENCE AND STYLE.
LANDSCAPE ARCHITECT
PERRY GUILLOT AND
I USED ARCHIVAL
PHOTOS TO RE-CREATE
THE FOOTPRINT OF
THE ORIGINAL GARDEN
IN SOUTHAMPTON.
PERRY THOUGHT OF
EVERY NUANCE:
"WHITE AND PALE-PINK
GARDEN ROSES
LIKE THE WASHED RED
BRICK OF THE HOUSE'S
FACADE. FORMAL
GARDENS FILLED WITH
STRONGER PURPLE-
BLUE SALVIA LINED WITH
LOW BOXWOODS."

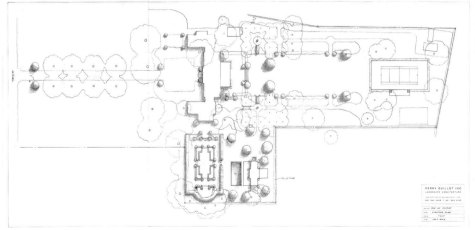

Our garden plan

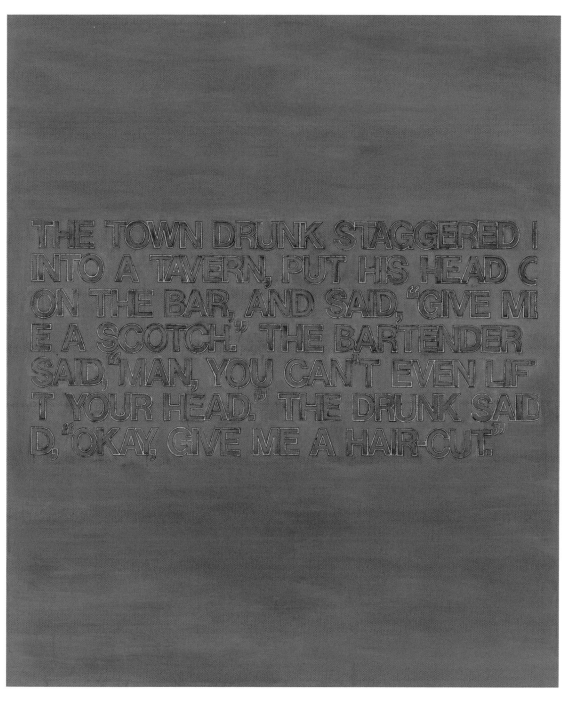

Richard Prince, Untitled (jokes), 2006

MY MOTHER, AN
ORGANIC GARDENER
SINCE THE SEVENTIES,
AND I SHARE A PASSION
FOR FRESH FLOWERS
AND VEGETABLES. I
CALL HER FOR ADVICE
EVERY YEAR.

RECENTLY PLANTED:
DELPHINIUM
LISIANTHUS
LAVENDER
BLUE CAMPANULA
CORNFLOWER
SWEET PEA
ZINNIA
DIANTHUS
SNAPDRAGON
COSMOS
RED CHERRY TOMATOES
BELL PEPPERS
ENGLISH CUCUMBERS
SQUASH
PURPLE ONION
LEMON VERBENA
OPAL BASIL
BRONZE FENNEL
CILANTRO & THYME
GREEN & PURPLE SHISO
CHERVIL

PATTERNED PORCELAIN

Order and disorder: There's something
strangely soothing about repeating patterns
and clusters of color and print. I see
them everywhere, especially in the porcelain
I collect—pieces I've received from my
mother and grandmother, found while traveling
or been given as presents from friends.

Armorial

Imari

Chinese export

Dutch delft

American spongeware

Wedgwood

THE GUEST ROOM—
I LIKE ROOMS THAT ARE
NOT TOO PERFECTLY
MATCHED. THE RED,
ORANGE AND TOUCH
OF GREEN THROW THINGS
OFF JUST A LITTLE IN OUR
GUEST BEDROOM. AND IT
MIXES ERAS AND STYLES:
GILT MIRROR FROM
MY PARENTS' HOME;
ENGLISH TOLE LAMP;
FLEA MARKET DRESSER
FROM FRANCE; INDIAN
HANDMADE DHURRIE, AND
D. PORTHAULT LINENS.

With my mom, Deucie and
Andy, Valley Forge, 1970

Simone and me, 1969

With Jamie, Simone & Donde, 1969

ON THE FARM

On any given day, if you stood at the front
door of Spring Meadow Farm, the home
I grew up in in Valley Forge, Pennsylvania,
you could hear a menagerie of animals,
including the occasional roar. My mom
and dad showed German shepherds,
and then there was Simone the Abyssinian,
the corgi Andy the Dandy, Mousseline
de Soie—aka Deucie—the poodle,
a multitude of turtles and lizards, Mackie
the macaw and Cracker the cockatoo.
There was also Tanya, my uncle's lion.
She only visited once in a while, thankfully.

REDBUD

Jeff Koons, Hanging Heart (Violet/Gold), 1994–2006

JEFF KOONS ON
HIS FAVORITE PEOPLE, PLACES AND THINGS

The contemporary artist finds inspiration in ordinary, everyday life.

The first thing you painted or sculpted...

Outside my kindergarten in York, Pennsylvania, there was a little wood shed for art, with Popsicle sticks and stuff. I enjoyed making things and coming home with what I'd made. Second, in our local Sunday paper, there was a section called Cappy Dick, about a sea captain, with a drawing for kids; you'd extend the line drawing on another piece of paper. You sent it in, and if you won, you'd get an encyclopedia. I did it every week. I never got first place, but I got second or third place. I remember drawing a scene with a sailfish jumping out of the water.

Person who inspires you . . .

A decade ago, I started to understand the depth of Picasso's work. Through the subjective, you go full circle to the objective. I was feeling stifled, and all of a sudden, I came into contact with someone who exercised to his fullest to interact with his freedom. I have a greater understanding of the objective... to live my life to its fullest.

Place that inspires you...

The city of Munich. I love the old Pinakothek museum. The Bouchers, the Rubenses, the da Vincis and Raphaels—I'm so profoundly moved.

Thing that inspires you...

Everyday objects. I had a friend and teacher, Ed Paschke, who shared where he got his source materials—everything is already here. You just have to open yourself up to it.

Art-wise, what reminds you of your childhood?

A gazing ball. It is an act of generosity for people to have one in their garden for their neighbors. You see a reflection of that spot, that place. And yet it reflects 360 degrees. It positions you in the universe and reaffirms your being; you move and it moves.

Let's free-associate with color...

Orange: pumpkin. **Blue:** sky.
Green: grass. **Purple:** spirituality.
Pink: sexuality. **Red:** fierce. **Yellow:** sun.
White: virginal. **Black:** basic.
Natural: beige-green. **Gold:** reflection.

And your favorite color...

I love turquoise. When I think of it, I'm aware that it was also my father's favorite. To me, it's rich, representing nature but at the same time representing a perception of blue.

St. Moritz, 2010

For traveling…

I love trains. I find them relaxing and a great
way to see beautiful countryside and listen
to great playlists, like this one from Lyor Cohen.

It's Like That Run DMC

It's My Thing EPMD

Rhymin' and Stealin' Beastie Boys

Bring the Noise Public Enemy

Ghetto Thang De La Soul

Electric Relaxation A Tribe Called Quest

It's Too Late Carole King

Sign o' the Times Prince

Hurt Johnny Cash

The Payback James Brown

He Hit Me (And It Felt Like a Kiss)
The Crystals

Faded Zhu

Strong London Grammar

Woman's Gotta Have It Bobby Womack

Reasons Earth, Wind & Fire

Fuck With Me You Know I Got It
Jay Z ft. Rick Ross

No Angel Beyoncé

Lost in the World Kanye West

Climax Usher

You're My Best Friend Queen

Oh La La The Faces

Happiness Is a Warm Gun The Beatles

Lively Up Yourself Bob Marley

WORK-LIFE BALANCE

It's one of the biggest topics of discussion in our office. Here are some extraordinary women who are constantly working to maintain this balance.

HILLARY RODHAM CLINTON, FORMER SECRETARY OF STATE

Why is work-life balance critical?

There is no right or wrong way to have a family—love is the only criteria. And there is no right or wrong way to build a career if you're following your dreams and providing for your family. There is a lot of debate among women on this issue, but it isn't a women's issue so much as a human issue and a family issue. It is a juggling act, and men and women alike need to find approaches that work for them. That approach may change over the course of their lives. You just need to figure out what works in your own life.

We also need policies to support women and men making these choices, because we all benefit when families are able to successfully balance responsibilities at home and at work.

How has that balance affected you personally?

When I was pregnant, I was the only female partner in a law firm in Arkansas. They'd never had a female partner, and certainly not a pregnant one. And they literally did not know what to do with me. I would walk down the corridor—getting more and more pregnant—and the men in the firm would look away. I thought to myself, "I'm just going to wait to see if anybody says anything to me about the fact that I'm going to have a baby." Nobody ever did.

And then on February 27, 1980, I gave birth to my daughter, Chelsea. I was in the hospital when one of my partners called to say congratulations. During our conversation, he asked, "When are you coming back to work?" And I said, "Oh, I don't know. Maybe in four months." That's how I created the firm's first-ever maternity leave policy. Years later, when I had a team of my own in the White House, we had mothers bringing bassinets to work. I encouraged parents to structure their hours and to work from home if necessary so that they could spend time with their children. One of the causes I've worked on for decades is early childhood development, especially helping parents become their kids' first teachers. That's only possible if they can devote that quality time.

CAROLINA HERRERA, DESIGNER

How do you manage time between work and life?

It is difficult to achieve a balance, but having discipline and being organized is a good start. I come to my office and I know that at that time, I will be working. When I arrive at home, I make sure that what I did at the office is left behind. My time at home spent with my family, friends and of course dogs is the time I love the most. You have to make sure you always have time to yourself.

What does a balanced life give us?

You must try for balance in order to feel fulfilled in different aspects of your life. Part of finding this balance in the context of work is to love what you do.

ARIANNA HUFFINGTON, PRESIDENT AND EDITOR-IN-CHIEF, THE HUFFINGTON POST MEDIA GROUP

What tools or processes have you put in place to balance work and life?

I have integrated certain practices into my day—meditation, walking, exercise—but the connection that conscious breathing gives me is something I can return to hundreds of times during the day in an instant.

Why do you think the balance is important?

It's tied in with the larger question of how we define success. Over time, society's notion of success has been reduced to money and power. But money and power by themselves are like a two-legged stool—you can balance on them for a while, but eventually you're going to topple over. The Western workplace culture—exported to many other parts of the world—is practically fueled by stress, sleep deprivation and burnout. Together, these elements are profoundly—and negatively—affecting our creativity, our productivity and our decision making.

ANGELICA CHEUNG,
EDITOR-IN-CHIEF, *VOGUE* CHINA

What are the benefits of a balanced lifestyle?
You gain better perspectives on life, become more understanding and tolerant. You also become more efficient, resourceful, capable and wise. Sometimes you need time away from the office to gain a better perspective on the challenges in front of you, and to find the right solutions.

What are some ways you keep a balance?
Every year I take two vacations with my family. During this period, I only check emails once a day and only respond to really important issues. As a result, my team takes more initiative, thus becoming more capable and responsible. Dropping my daughter off at school every day—that is a very valued part of my routine.

AZRA A. KHALFAN,
CEO, PLAQUES BY AZRA

What does a better balance give you?
"It creates harmony, allowing me to exercise my full potential. In running our business for 17 years, I have traveled, spent precious times with my family and volunteered for causes I believe in. Taking this all into account helps me gain a better perspective—I stay focused on the positive and am grateful for what I have."

BRIGITTE KLEINE,
PRESIDENT, TORY BURCH

What has finding a better balance taught you?
I believe the best leaders truly enjoy life outside of work. Having a great team and empowering them is critical to finding balance, which leads to better decision making both at work and at home. And finding that ultimate balance is ongoing; accept that you continue to learn as you go along.

DINA POWELL, PRESIDENT,
THE GOLDMAN SACHS FOUNDATION

What are your thoughts on women finding the balance?
Women are masters of balance. Through our foundation's partnership with the Tory Burch Foundation and other partners, we see women around the world doing more than you can imagine. Women build businesses and careers, care for their families and then invest their time and success in their communities.

How do you balance motherhood and work?
I try my best to make sure my daughters understand the work that I do and involve them, including having the opportunity to introduce them to amazing individuals. I'm fortunate to work with many women entrepreneurs around the world, who give my daughters remarkable role models.

BRIGITTE AT OUR SHOW, 2013.

New York City, 2011

Pink button-down shirts, rolled-up khakis and espadrilles—this was my father's summer uniform while he rode around the farm on his tractor, listening to baseball games on a transistor radio. That memory epitomizes true style to me. Pink is an old-fashioned color—in the best way. The palest shade works against navy, red, orange, coral, olive or white. It makes me think of Henri Matisse, Agnes Martin and Lucio Fontana. I love pink, and as I write this book, I am in the process of finding just the right shade in linen for the couch in my bedroom.

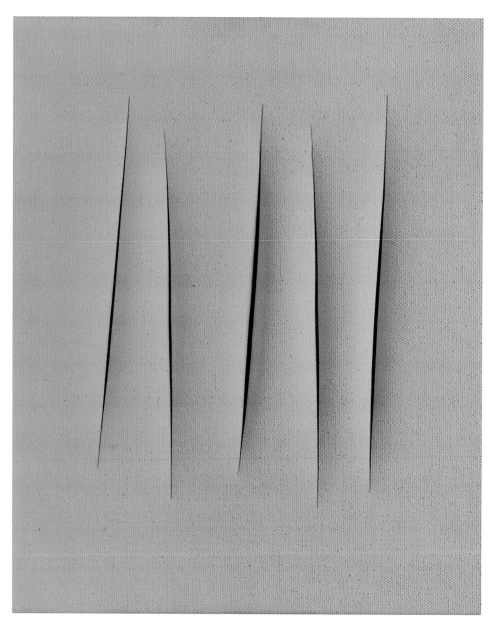

Lucio Fontana, Concetto Spaziale, Attese, 1964

SATURDAY LUNCHES

Summers are the best time to have friends
over for lunches that stretch into the late
afternoon or evening. No one is in a hurry.
Tables, like rooms and collections, can
tell a story. I like the modernity of the striped
Italian glasses and Puiforcat flatware
against the Indian block-print linens and
floral settings from D. Porthault and
Heinrich & Co., opposite. My mother gave me
porcelain birds and the majolica tureen—
perfect for fresh-cut hyacinths.

DAVID HICKS

The designer, above, in a pink blazer
and moccasins; a room that's simple
but chic—a bowl of pineapples and
a graphic painting. Easy and glamorous.

As with most great artists, he could
extract a wonderful idea from almost
anything he looked at. The pink walls
of a client's living room in Portugal,
for example, were the same shade as the
lining of a thank-you note's envelope.

MY FIRST FRAGRANCE

My mother keeps a tray on her vanity with
some of her favorite fragrances and vintage
perfume bottles. When I was young, I used
to try them all on (at the same time, of course),
and then get thrown directly in the bath.

Vetiver and peony evoke powerful
memories for me of my father and mother.
My father, and now my brothers, always
wore vetiver. Peonies bring me back to all the
summer days I spent as my mother's assistant
gardener. When I created my first fragrance
with Estée Lauder, I hoped to capture all
of these memories that are still so vibrant.

I love the alchemy of fragrance, from the
actual ingredients to the bottle's architecture.
We wanted a mix of tomboy and feminine,
not too earthy, not too sweet. The bottle's
fretwork was inspired by Chippendale
chairs; the lines and beveled edges informed
by Donald Judd and Josef Albers.

When we named our lip colors and tints,
I spent time remembering some of our
favorite sayings growing up. My mother says
"Divine" in nearly every sentence, and
"Pas du tout" comes from a French saying
my father loved.

CREATING OUR FIRST
FRAGRANCE WAS A LOT
LIKE DESIGNING A
COLLECTION: TRIAL
AND ERROR WITH
DIFFERENT INGREDIENTS,
AND COLLABORATING
WITH A GREAT TEAM,
LIKE ESTÉE LAUDER WITH
LEONARD LAUDER AND
VERONIQUE GABAI-PINSKY.

New York City, 2013

LEONARD LAUDER ON FINE ART & PEOPLE

The Chairman Emeritus of the Estée Lauder Companies discusses Picasso, people and Paris.

**What scent or fragrance reminds you of
your childhood?**
Youth Dew—the first fragrance Mrs. Estée Lauder
created and wore forever. It reminds me of motherly love.

**If you could own only one piece of artwork,
what would it be?**
The portrait of Gertrude Stein by Pablo Picasso in the
Met. Picasso took an unattractive woman and made
her into the power that she was with his brushstrokes.

**If you could spend one hour with any artist—
any time period—who would it be?**
I'd spend more than one hour with many artists.
Like Jasper Johns or Bob Rauschenberg or Brice
Marden. Every artist—I love talking to them. Everyone
comes up with such a different point of view. It's like the
creation of a mosaic.

Your favorite room in your favorite museum...
Oskar Schlemmer's painting *Bauhaus Stairway*. It was
on the steps of the early MoMA building at 11 West 53rd
Street—now named after my brother. As a kid, I used
to go to MoMA two or three times a week and, going in
and out, I'd always see that painting. Our first office,
where I worked for many years, was in the Fifth Avenue
building across from MoMA. I'd slip across the street
and have lunch in the cafeteria, and I'd see it every day.
It's a part of me now.

Best piece of advice you ever received...
My Italian isn't very good, but here's a translation
of a Venetian saying: Before you speak, be silent.

**How do you build your team? What do you look for
in people?**
Do they burn? Do they have passion and compassion?
Then they have it.

Moment you're most proud of...
Every time I see someone from my company, who has
grown up in the company or made progress, come up with
something great. To see how they've risen and grown.

What's your favorite color?
Light blue—that's the color of the Estée Lauder
packaging. It's soft and embracing. Whenever I see
it in a room, I heave a sigh of relief. The other color
I love is a lemon yellow in combination with white trim.
It gives me a feeling of relaxation.

And what inspires you?
Traveling, and most particularly traveling to Paris.
The French are all about taste. Every little thing
has a touch. When I go to someone's home for dinner,
the fact that they put the roll wrapped in a napkin
on a plate. Only the French do that. All those little
niceties. What inspires me are the little details
that say "I care."

HOW DO YOU TAKE
A MOROCCAN HAT AND
PAINTINGS BY ÉDOUARD
MANET AND HENRI
MATISSE AND MAKE
THE COMBINATION
WORK? RESORT 2014
CELEBRATED THE SPIRIT
OF THAT MIX, IN WHICH
INSPIRATIONS PLAYED
OFF ONE ANOTHER
IN DIFFERENT WAYS.

Henri Matisse, Anemones and Chinese Vase, 1922

"MIXING COLORFUL PATTERNS, WORKING IN TEXTILES,
TRANSFORMING SPACES SO THERE'S A SENSE OF DEPTH—
THAT WAS THE HALLMARK OF MATISSE'S WORK."

– JUDITH DOLKART, CHIEF CURATOR, THE BARNES FOUNDATION

COVER INSPIRATION: BOOKS,
BELOW, FOUND ON
THE DESIGN TEAM'S SHELF.

———

WILLEM DE KOONING
HAD A DIFFERENT TAKE
ON THE 1950S IDEAL
OF THE AMERICAN WOMAN.
THIS ONE: *MARILYN
MONROE*, 1954.

Willem de Kooning, Marilyn Monroe, 1954

The Classics

My first concert was the Grateful Dead,
when I was in ninth grade. I went with
my brothers and some high school friends
in Philadelphia. My taste in music is eclectic,
and there's nothing better than discovering
a new artist—hip-hop, classical or rock.
On our blog, we post regular playlists, like
this one by music supervisor Randall Poster.

Back in My Arms Again The Supremes

Beast of Burden The Rolling Stones

Can I Kick It? A Tribe Called Quest

Carey Joni Mitchell

Doctor My Eyes Jackson Browne

Everyday People Sly & the Family Stone

Fool Yourself Little Feat

Hard to Handle Otis Redding

Heart of Gold Neil Young

Jamming Bob Marley

Just Like Heaven The Cure

Leopard-Skin Pill-Box Hat Bob Dylan

Lola The Kinks

Mathematics Mos Def

Ripple Grateful Dead

She's Got You Patsy Cline

Tell Me Something Good Rufus & Chaka Khan

Tupelo Honey Van Morrison

Wanted Man Johnny Cash

Wouldn't It Be Nice The Beach Boys

Young Americans David Bowie

Yours Love Dolly Parton & Porter Wagoner

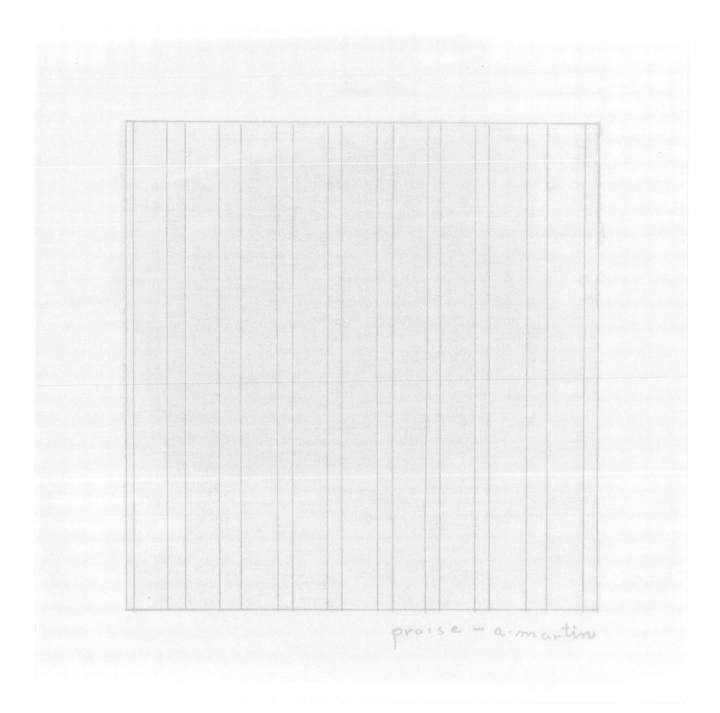

Agnes Martin, Praise, from the Rubber Stamp Portfolio, 1976

"AGNES MARTIN'S PAINTINGS
LOOK LIKE THEY'RE ACTUALLY BLUSHING."
—JEANNE GREENBERG ROHATYN, GALLERIST, SALON 94

Valley Forge, 1969

Mother's Best Advice

Every year on the blog, we have shared the wisdom of moms. My mother says,
"The glass is always half full," "Always look for the positive in every situation" and
"When one door closes, another one opens."

"TO CONTINUE
MY EDUCATION."

—CHRISTY TURLINGTON BURNS

"MY MOM HAS ALWAYS
SAID, 'YOU HAVE TO
BE YOUR OWN BEST
FRIEND.' WHEN I WAS
A KID, I DIDN'T
UNDERSTAND THIS."

—MINDY KALING

"ALWAYS CHECK
THE SEAMS OF
A GARMENT TO
SEE IF IT'S MADE
WELL. AND ALWAYS
BE RESPONSIBLE
WITH WORK."

—CHRISTENE BARBERICH

"THINK FOR YOURSELF."

—AMY ASTLEY

"NEVER WHINE.
GET ANGRY, YELL,
SLAM A DOOR
IF YOU MUST, BUT
NEVER WHINE.
IT'S UNBECOMING."

—BRIDGET FOLEY

"DON'T FORGET
YOUR MANNERS."

—AMANDA BROOKS

"THE WAY TO A
MAN'S HEART
IS THROUGH HIS
STOMACH; WEAR
ALL THE HAREM
PANTS YOU WANT."

—LEANDRA MEDINE

"MY MOTHER'S BEST
ADVICE HOLDS TRUE
IN BOTH WORK
AND PERSONAL
LIFE. IT'S EXCEEDINGLY
SIMPLE—BUT HARD
TO ABIDE BY: 'GIVE IT
YOUR ALL. HAVE AN
OPINION. AND DON'T
BE AFRAID TO STAND
UP FOR WHAT IS YOURS
AND RIGHT. BUT
BE FORGIVING—
TO YOURSELF AND
TO OTHERS—AS WELL.'"

—EVA CHEN

"MY MOM FINDS A
JOIE DE VIVRE
IN THE EVERYDAY.
SHE TAUGHT ME
TO SEE THE FUN AND
CREATIVITY IN
WHATEVER I'M DOING."

—DARCY MILLER NUSSBAUM

"FROM MY
GRANDMOTHER:
'YOUTH GIVES
YOU ENERGY TO
MAKE MEMORIES
TO RELAX WITH
WHEN YOU'RE OLD,
SO MAKE THE
MOST YOU CAN!'"

—MARIO GRAUSO

"WHILE TEACHING
ME HOW TO SEW,
SHE TRAINED
ME TO MAKE EVERY
GARMENT AS
PERFECT ON THE
INSIDE AS ON
THE EXTERIOR.
THIS HOLDS TRUE
FOR EVERYTHING
ONE ATTEMPTS
IN LIFE."

—SALLY SINGER

"ALWAYS START
WITH KINDNESS."

—ROBBIE MYERS

"SHE GAVE ME A LOT
OF GOOD ADVICE, BUT
ATTACHED TO EACH
WAS THE CONSTANT
REMINDER, 'DON'T
SHOOT YOUR MOUTH
OFF.' I THINK THIS WAS
THE MESSAGE SHE
WANTED TO IMPART."

—DAVID NETTO

"THAT FASHION
IS SUCH A GREAT
FORM OF
SELF-EXPRESSION."

—VERA WANG

"TRUST YOUR
INSTINCTS."

—KRISTINA O'NEILL

"SIT UP STRAIGHT."

—JOHN DERIAN

"THAT BEAUTY IS
PASSED ON THROUGH
LOVE. THE MORE
YOU LOVE SOMEONE,
AND THE BETTER
YOU TREAT THEM, THE
MORE BEAUTIFUL
THEY BECOME FROM
THE INSIDE OUT."

—VERONICA WEBB

"THAT WORK
WAS NO MORE
IMPORTANT
THAN YOUR
HOME, YOUR
FRIENDS, YOUR
FAMILY, EVEN
YOUR CLOSET."

—FRANCESCA DIMATTIO

Taiwan, 2011

"He who binds to himself a joy
Does the winged life destroy
He who kisses the joy as it flies
Lives in eternity's sunrise."

—WILLIAM BLAKE

R

ed was a subtle but powerful part of my childhood. Our home in Valley Forge had pops of red here and there: the clay tennis court where my mother taught us to play; the runner that went up our front stairs; her velvet porter's chair at the bottom of the staircase; and the ribbons she decorated the house with at Christmas. My friends and family carry a red ribbon for good luck. It's a tradition my grandmother Lillian started. When my mother brought my brother Robert home from the hospital, my grandmother tied a ribbon to the bottom of his crib to keep him safe. Any time my boys go away, I tie a red ribbon to their suitcase or on their wrist.

OUR FARM, DECKED FOR THE HOLIDAYS.

MY FAVORITE PLACE

We moved into Spring Meadow Farm
in the middle of a snowstorm, right around
Christmas. I was a few months old, and my
parents pulled me down the driveway in a sled.
There was no electricity in the house that day,
so my father built fires in every room.

That first Christmas, all our decorations
were still in boxes, so my parents cut down
a small tree and covered it with red bows.
My mom loves all holidays and traditions.
It would start at Thanksgiving. The house
was packed with friends and family, and the
party lasted through New Year's Eve. Inside
and out, the house was swathed in garlands,
wreaths and ornaments. Every year for our
holiday party invitations, she hand-painted red
ribbons and a garland on a sketch of our home.

RIGHT: THE DARK,
ROMANTIC PALETTE
IRVING PENN MASTERED
WITH HIS *3 POPPIES*,
1969—A DEEP MAROON
WE HAVE USED IN OUR
OWN COLLECTION.

JANE BIRKIN ON MOVIES, MUSIC AND WHAT'S IN HER BAG

The blog team spoke to the style icon and
epitome of cool French insouciance in 2011.

Best advice you've ever received...
"Smile and the world smiles with you.
Cry and you cry alone."

Favorite movie...
The Producers by Mel Brooks,
Billy Wilder's *La Garçonnière* and, oh,
Ingmar Bergman's *The Silence*.

Soundtrack of your life...
John Barry's *The Lion in Winter*.

Favorite designer...
Serge Gainsbourg!

Your style is best described as...
Personal!

What's in your bag...
My life.

A wink or a smile...
A smile.

Irving Penn, 3 Poppies, Arab Chief, New York, 1969

श्री ओरेडायक देवजी (श्री भैरव जी)

I take pictures everywhere
I go... Flowers on a
Rajasthani temple, 2009 translated
for Spring 2013

THE PINKY-RED BACKDROP, ABOVE,
OF OUR DEAUVILLE-INSPIRED
SPRING 2012 RUNWAY MADE THE
COLLECTION POP.

A TUNIC AND A TULIP PRINT,
SUMMER 2012.

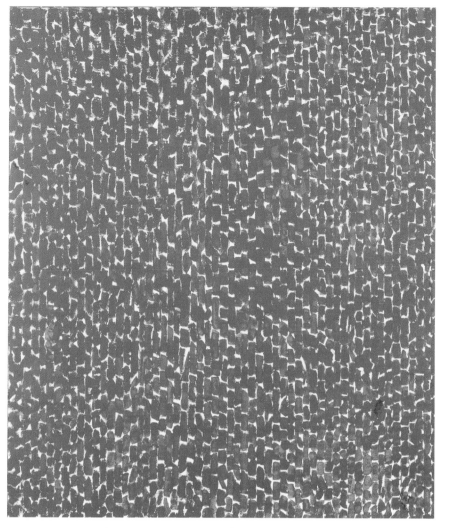

Alma Thomas, Antares, 1972

Laurie Simmons,
The Love Doll: Day 31 (Geisha), 2011

THELMA GOLDEN & JEANNE GREENBERG ROHATYN ON ART

The Director and Chief Curator of The Studio Museum in Harlem
and the Founder of Salon 94 share insights.

How did you become interested in art?

Thelma: When I was eight, some friends gave me the board game Masterpiece. I was intrigued by the cards that were reproductions of great works of art. Shortly after, in fifth grade, I had an amazing art history teacher, Lucille Buck. That was the beginning.

Jeanne: I played Masterpiece to learn about art auctions. But for me, that aha moment was at 12, when my father took me to Art Basel. We visited Ernst Beyeler, and in his office he had a small Cézanne *Bathers*. I wanted to take it home and stare at it all day long. We then went by train to Colmar to see the Grünewald Altarpiece. I like the idea of a pilgrimage to see a work of art—of finding it through some kind of an adventure. My galleries are a little off the beaten track as a result.

Thelma: That's interesting. My greatest adolescent battle with my parents was my desire to take the subway into Manhattan to see museums. When I was finally given permission, my pilgrimages were from Queens to the Museum of Modern Art. It's my hope that we might be able to provide that for a kid—to come in to The Studio Museum in Harlem and find a real refuge.

Jeanne, tell us the story about you, Andy Warhol and the now-iconic banana.

Jeanne: In 1974, Warhol came for his opening at my father's gallery and stayed at our house. He had sent his *Mao Wallpaper* for the exhibition. Instead of putting it in the gallery, my father wallpapered our guest bathroom, almost as if a joke to say "Look, Andy, I need paintings, not wallpaper." Warhol hung out in that room all night, and I stayed at his side. In between signing Campbell soup cans, he drew me a banana. It wasn't until college that I understood its significance as The Velvet Underground logo.

Thelma: You can encounter art at one point in your life, when it has one meaning, and then over time, your understanding changes.

Which women artists deserve more credit?

Thelma: There are whole generations of women—from 20- to 90-somethings—making fierce, bold, interesting work. The late Alma Thomas is a great example. Though she was the first-ever fine arts graduate from Howard University, she spent four decades teaching in Washington, DC, before beginning her career as an artist at 69. She then made some of the most amazing abstract paintings of the 20th century.

Jeanne: Thomas lays the groundwork for many artists today—Julie Mehretu's abstracts are indebted to Thomas. Laurie Simmons is doing her strongest work today, as if she is reemerging. Both her daughters, Lena and Grace Dunham, are out of the house. She has the freedom now to take all of the risks that she taught her children to take.

Alma Thomas and Laurie Simmons both have colorful work. What are *your* thoughts on color?

Jeanne: Every decade has a defining palette. The Sixties were psychedelic, the Eighties neon. There's a Frank Stella painting in Seventies green and yellow; I thought of the Brady Bunch's living room or Mary Tyler Moore's wardrobe—cultural things that happened at that time.

Thelma: Color is a key to understanding how artists think about their work. The palette of the world influences what we are, what we know and who we are.

Jeanne: Artists have taken ownership of certain colors—Yves Klein's blue, Robert Ryman's white, Glenn Ligon's black.

Thelma: I am lucky that the richness of my own experience allows me to understand the world through color in cultural and political terms.

Jeanne: Absolutely. It's funny—I don't think of you as a color but rather in terms of a patchwork of colors that make up patterns.

Thelma: Maybe that's because I live with an amazing artist and fashion designer, my husband Duro Olowu. His genius is in mixing color, pattern and texture. The fact that I get to wear a Duro design has given me a greater sense of the joy of color.

l'essentiel est que je communique

CLOCKWISE FROM FAR LEFT: NICK AND HENRY, PHOTOGRAPHED BY ARTHUR ELGORT, 2000; A PAINTING I FOUND IN A FLEA MARKET; SAWYER AND ME, 2007; A MESSAGE FROM THE ARTIST BEN, 1970; A CHINESE PAINTING IN MY LIBRARY; TAMU MACPHERSON, IN FALL 2012, PHOTOGRAPHED FOR THE BLOG.

FROM LEFT, TOP ROW: AVIE AND GIGI MORTIMER; WITH JAMIE ALEXANDER TISCH AND ANGIE HARMON; WITH PERRI PELTZ, GIGI AND AUTUMN HANNA VANDEHEI. SECOND ROW: JODIE SHELLOW; SARAH LANDMAN SCHWARZ; ROBERT AND ELENA ALLBRITTON (BELOW); ESTHER SONG; MOLLY GOWEN GROOME. THIRD ROW: LOUISE AND VINCE CAMUTO; WITH DR. SAMANTHA BOARDMAN, DEREK BLASBERG, VERA WANG AND LAUREN SANTO DOMINGO; MARJORIE GUBELMANN, TICO MUGRABI AND SAMANTHA; AUTUMN AND JIM VANDEHEI. FOURTH ROW: WITH JEANNE GREENBERG ROHATYN AND WILLIAM NORWICH; MARCIA MISHAAN; WITH ELIZABETH LINDEMANN, MICHAEL MEAGHER, TODD MEISTER AND DANIEL ROMUALDEZ.

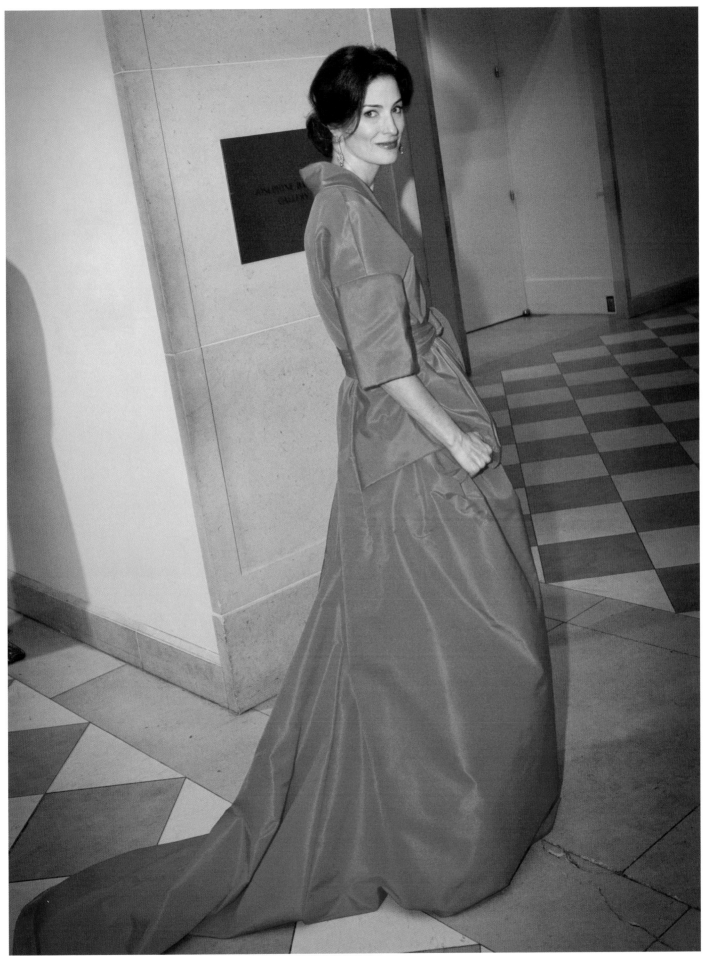

Marina Rust, The Met Gala, 2011

It

GIVES   ME

GREAT

PLEASURE.

CECIL

BEATON.

My parents, Maine, 1972

Hawaii, 2013

Tokyo, 2010

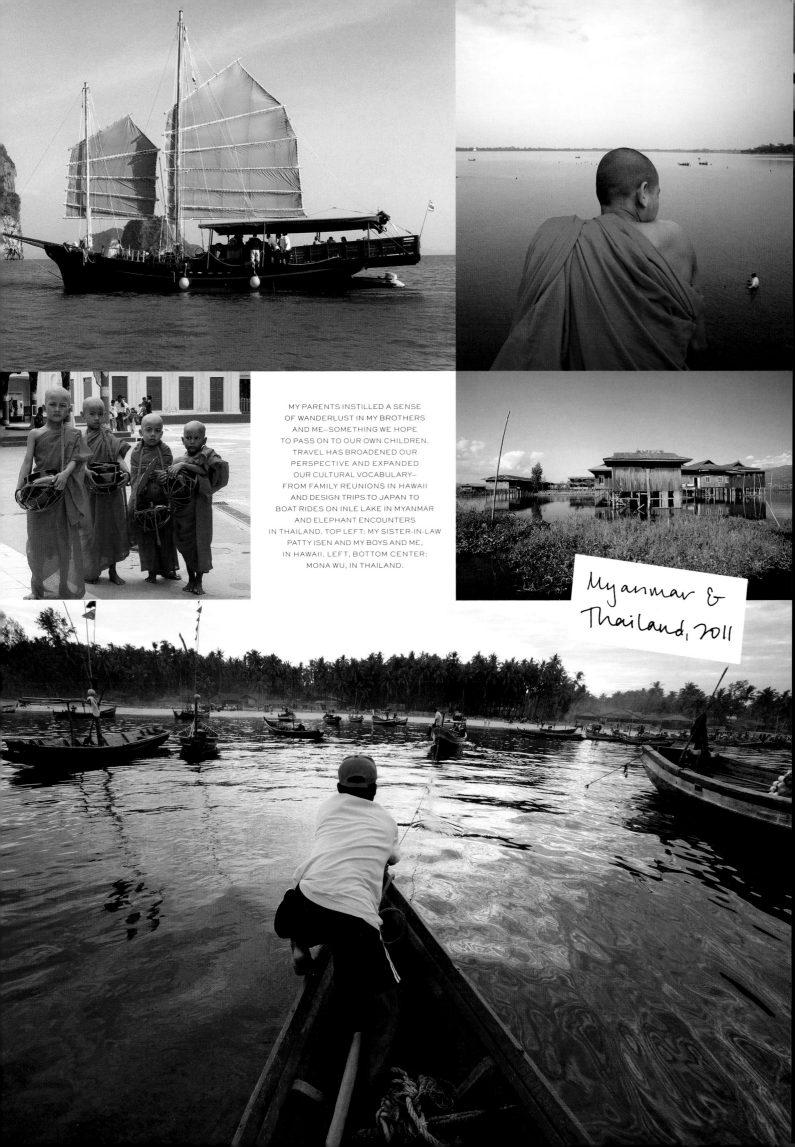

MY PARENTS INSTILLED A SENSE
OF WANDERLUST IN MY BROTHERS
AND ME—SOMETHING WE HOPE
TO PASS ON TO OUR OWN CHILDREN.
TRAVEL HAS BROADENED OUR
PERSPECTIVE AND EXPANDED
OUR CULTURAL VOCABULARY—
FROM FAMILY REUNIONS IN HAWAII
AND DESIGN TRIPS TO JAPAN TO
BOAT RIDES ON INLE LAKE IN MYANMAR
AND ELEPHANT ENCOUNTERS
IN THAILAND. TOP LEFT: MY SISTER-IN-LAW
PATTY ISEN AND MY BOYS AND ME,
IN HAWAII. LEFT, BOTTOM CENTER:
MONA WU, IN THAILAND.

Myanmar &
Thailand, 2011

Porto Ercole, 2008

"I wandered lonely as a cloud
That floats on high o'er vales and hills,
When all at once I saw a crowd,
A host, of golden daffodils."
—WILLIAM WORDSWORTH

Yellow is optimistic. There is a picture of my mother wearing a Pucci bathing suit in our backyard that perfectly captures the ease and glamour of the 1970s—it's a favorite of my team's. Yellow fits my mother's personality—she is the most optimistic person I know. There is that perfect shade that is very light, almost the color of lemon ice. I like it paired back to navy, white or olive, and I especially love it against gold.

Valley Forge, 1969

THE BACKYARD

We lived outside at our farm. My parents
always entertained—big, small, but
always with family. My father loved
to barbecue—hamburgers, steak, chicken
and fresh vegetables (from my mother's
garden). We lit gas torches that lined
the iron fence around the pool and
the front of the house. Children were
everywhere—our house was home
base for all of our friends.

MY FIRST HANDBAG
AND MY FIRST HAIRCUT.
MY DAD HAD JUST
TAKEN MY BROTHERS
AND ME TO THE
BARBER. I GOT THE
SAME HAIRCUT AS
THE BOYS. NEEDLESS
TO SAY, MY MOTHER
WAS NOT THRILLED.

MILTON AVERY'S
BRIGHT *INTERLUDE*.

———————

LEFT: NICK, HENRY
AND ME AT THE
BEACH, 2000,
BY ARTHUR ELGORT.

Milton Avery, Interlude, 1960

THE MARGARITA

INGREDIENTS
1½ oz tequila
1½ oz Cointreau
1½ oz freshly squeezed lime juice
Ice
Slice of lime

DIRECTIONS
Fill shaker with ice and add tequila,
Cointreau and lime juice.
Shake vigorously and pour into glass.
Add a slice of lime.

THIS ICONIC PHOTOGRAPH FROM THE SIXTIES HANGS IN THE HALLWAY OF OUR OFFICE. IT REMINDS US TO UNWIND NOW AND AGAIN.
MY FRIEND BARBARA LIBERMAN, A PSYCHOANALYST, SAYS, "THE BALANCE OF HARD WORK AND THE NEED TO REPLENISH IS CRITICAL. TAKING A MOMENT
TO RELAX AND ESCAPE, EVEN FOR JUST A DAY, CAN SUPPLY THE NEEDED PERSPECTIVE TO REENERGIZE AND FUEL CREATIVITY."

Gerhard Richter, Abstract Painting (812), 1994

FAMILY TRIPS

Friends and a camera. The children try
to out-flip, -dive, -ski each other, so we are
always outside or in the water.
On one fishing trip in the Bahamas,
above left, Gigi Mortimer and my boys found
it funny that I caught a yellow fish that
matched my windbreaker.

CLOCKWISE FROM TOP LEFT: GIGI AND ME; JAMIE,
ROBERT AND LEONARD; NICK MID-FLIP; MY BOYS
IN MUSTIQUE; MY SISTER-IN-LAW NICOLE.

SPRING 2013

Before every show, our hairstylist Eugene
Souleiman, stylist Tabitha Simmons and
I have a conversation about the runway story.
Eugene, who created messy fishtail braids
for Spring 2013, said it best: "The girl has
been traveling and these braids have fallen
a little apart. I wanted to see the little
imperfections—there's a sensuality to it."

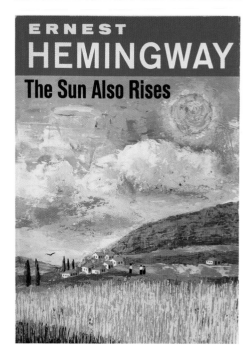

FROM LEFT, TOP ROW: STEFANO TONCHI;
AMY FINE COLLINS; WITH THE TENNIS GROUP, TOP
ROW: KITTY SHERRILL, ARIADNE CALVO-PLATERO,
PERRI PELTZ, GIGI MORTIMER, RENEE ROCKEFELLER,
JENNY CONANT; BOTTOM ROW: PEGGY SIEGEL,
CRISTINA CUOMO AND SARA AYRES; BRIDGET FOLEY;
BRIGITTE, PAOLO RIVA AND ROBERT; LEONARD
AND ERIKA LOPEZ; RENEE. SECOND ROW: ELLIE
BERLIN; WITH KIERNAN SHIPKA AND RASHIDA JONES;
KARA ROSS; WITH LAWRENCE LIBUNAO; CHRISTINA
SMITH; RENA SINDI ABBOUD. THIRD ROW, INSET: KATE
ETTER; CLAUDE WASSERSTEIN; LYOR COHEN; DARBY
DUNN AND HER SON TEDDY; KRISTIN BIDDLE;
WITH RASHIDA; CARYN ZUCKER; CRISTINA CUOMO.
FOURTH ROW: TABITHA SIMMONS; RACHEL
HOVNANIAN; HAYLEY BOESKY; ELISA DAL POS
(BELOW); MEG DOEPKE; WITH JEN NILLES AND
GORDON HULL; ELIZABETH SALTZMAN; FRANCES
PENNINGTON; ELIZABETH LINDEMANN;
LISA JACKSON; DANA TAYLOR.

GREAT ADVICE

My team and I always ask people to share their best advice or guidance
that they have received from others.

"BE OVERLY CRITICAL OF ALL THE LITTLE DETAILS—EVERYONE WILL EVENTUALLY NOTICE."

—JESSICA ALBA

"SEE THINGS IN A NEW WAY. BE UNIQUE, HAVE A VISION AND A POINT OF VIEW."

—JOE ZEE

"FIND WHO AND WHAT YOU LOVE."

— CHARLIE ROSE

"DAVID REMNICK ONCE TOLD ME WHEN I HAD JUST STARTED WORKING FOR *THE NEW YORKER* AND HE WAS A STAFF WRITER, 'NEVER APOLOGIZE FOR WORK IN ADVANCE.'"

— VANESSA FRIEDMAN

"DIANA VREELAND TOLD ME THAT ONE SHOULD HAVE DISCIPLINE IN LIFE. SHE WAS RIGHT."

—MARISA BERENSON

"BE NICE TO EVERYONE, NOT JUST UPPER MANAGEMENT. BONUS: YOU DON'T HAVE THE BIRD'S-EYE VIEW. TRUST IN OTHER PEOPLE'S GUIDANCE."

—ARIEL FOXMAN

"GREAT COMPANIES ARE MANAGED BY PEOPLE WHOSE EMOTIONS AND PASSIONS ARE TIED UP IN THEM."

—MILLARD DREXLER

"ASK QUESTIONS. NO ONE'S BORN KNOWING EVERYTHING ABOUT EVERYTHING."

—CINDI LEIVE

"FROM MY FORMER BOSS, CALVIN KLEIN: 'START YOUR OWN COMPANY. YOU CAN DO IT. IT WILL BE GREAT.'"

—NARCISO RODRIGUEZ

"LEARN AS MUCH AS YOU CAN, THEN FORGET IT ALL."

— CINDY SHERMAN

"LEADERS ASK QUESTIONS AND INSPIRE; MANAGERS TELL PEOPLE WHAT TO DO."

— ERIC SCHMIDT

"EMBRACE AMBITION."

— JANE ROSENTHAL

"FOLLOW YOUR OWN NORTH STAR. FOLLOW YOUR PASSION AND BE UNRELENTING."

—GLEN SENK

"LEARN HOW TO TELL YOUR STORY. GET YOUR ELEVATOR PITCH DOWN. IF YOU'RE SPEAKING, GET IT UNDER THREE MINUTES; IF YOU'RE WRITING, IN THE FIRST PARAGRAPH, EVEN IN THE FIRST LINE. TELL IT WITHOUT JARGON. TELL IT BOLDLY AND CONFIDENTLY AND WELL."

— ANNE FULENWIDER

"NEVER IMPORT OTHER PEOPLE'S LIMITATIONS."

—GAYLE TZEMACH LEMMON

"THREE THINGS: THE HARDER YOU WORK, THE LUCKIER YOU GET. MAKE YOURSELF INDISPENSABLE. AND IF IT WAS EASY, EVERYONE WOULD BE DOING IT."

—NATALIE MASSENET

"FROM THE POET RENÉ CHAR: *'IMPOSE TA CHANCE, SERRE TON BONHEUR ET VA VERS TON RISQUE. À TE REGARDER ILS S'HABITUERONT.'* OR, LOOSELY TRANSLATED, 'PUSH YOUR LUCK, SEIZE YOUR HAPPINESS, AND TAKE YOUR CHANCES. WATCHING YOU, THEY'LL FOLLOW.'"

—PIERRE-YVES ROUSSEL

ANTOINE DE SAINT-EXUPÉRY

The Little Prince

THE LITTLE PRINCE–EQUALLY IMPORTANT FOR ADULTS AS IT IS FOR CHILDREN.

THE FIRST THING YOU NOTICE IN INDIA
IS THE COLOR. VIBRANT AND MORE DIVERSE
THAN YOU CAN FATHOM. AND THEN YOU SEE
THE EMBROIDERY, EMBELLISHMENT, PRINTS
AND TEXTILES. EVERY FLOWER, FRUIT, STREET,
BUILDING AND DOORWAY HAS A DETAIL THAT
IS WORTH PHOTOGRAPHING. EVEN THE BUSES
ARE PAINTED BEAUTIFULLY. COLOR IS
EVERYWHERE. ABOVE LEFT: SNAKES AND
CHARMS OUTSIDE THE AMBER FORT.

SUCCESS IS
COUNTED SWEETEST

Success is counted sweetest
By those who ne'er succeed.
To comprehend a nectar
Requires sorest need.

Not one of all the purple Host
Who took the Flag today
Can tell the definition
So clear of Victory

As he defeated—dying—
On whose forbidden ear
The distant strains of triumph
Burst agonized and clear.

—EMILY DICKINSON

Hawaii, 2013

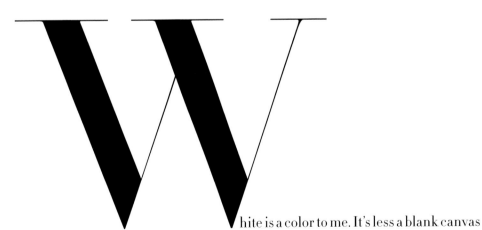

White is a color to me. It's less a blank canvas than a statement of its own. Pure and elegant. I grew up in a white stucco Georgian home, and we spent all our time on the white lattice-and-fretwork porch, playing games and watching storms roll in. That fretwork has inspired many collections and is a signature detail in our boutiques. White works with anything, but I love it with blue, green and ivory. And, of course, it stands on its own... I can't resist classic tennis whites.

Philadelphia, 1950s

Being a gentleman is not a part-time job.
—Buddy Robinson

OUR BUDDY VALUES

We show up with
HONESTY + KINDNESS

We work with
PASSION + HUMILITY

We act with
INTEGRITY + COMPASSION

We lead with
EXCELLENCE + HUMOR

BUDDY

My father, Buddy, was unique. He taught me about elegance, in every sense of the word: the way you treat people, the way you live your life, the way you dress. He had an appetite for beautiful things and, with my mother, had collections from around the world.

A true dandy, he should have been a fashion designer. He customized his own suits and cuff links, and he designed jewelry for my mother. He covered his gold Zippo lighter with sentimental charms, and I now wear it as a pendant. He lined his dinner jackets with Hermès scarves and wore Gucci loafers before it was de rigueur. At the same time, he was happy riding his tractor around our farm. And he was a collector—the ashtrays from various hotels he stayed at I now use as soap dishes.

He had impeccable manners and limitless compassion. Combine this with a wicked and dry sense of humor—irresistible. His charm drew people to him. He was endlessly patient and even-keeled. I definitely get my sense of calm from him—and it has helped me immeasurably at critical points in my personal life and at work.

When we were talking about the kind of culture we wanted at our company, we kept going back to the way Buddy, and my mother, lived. With kindness, integrity, humor and a sense of pride in ourselves and our work. Soon after he passed away in 2007, we started referring to our core culture and values as "Buddy"—and it stuck. Knowing him, he would absolutely be amused.

THERE IS A METICULOUS ATTENTION TO DETAIL AND SYMMETRY IN ARCHITECTURE,
FROM MOROCCAN TEMPLES TO THE 18TH-CENTURY GEORGIAN HOMES IN PHILADELPHIA. IT ALL APPEALS
TO THE PERFECTIONIST IN ME (AN EYE I GET FROM MY MOTHER). I CAN SEE IF SOMETHING IS ONE-
EIGHTEENTH OF AN INCH OFF. CLOCKWISE FROM OPPOSITE PAGE: DELPHINIUMS AND FERNS IN SCULPTED
VASES; MOROCCAN DETAIL; BUDDHIST TEMPLES IN MYANMAR; SPRING 2014 BEADWORK; IN INDIA, 2009.

Carlos in our NYC office, 2014

CARLOS MOTA
ON STORIED HOTELS

The international stylist loves places
with an interesting history.

Villa Treville
Positano, Italy

Once the private house of Franco Zeffirelli.
You feel like you are in the 1960s
and that you could run into Elizabeth
Taylor at any moment.

Hotel Nord-Pinus
Tangier, Morocco

Like you're staying in someone's home.
Each room has different antiques
and fabrics.

Hotel Riad Madani
Marrakech, Morocco

One of the largest private gardens
in the middle of the Medina.

Hotel Fasano
São Paulo, Brazil

It is modern, chic, masculine and sexy.
One of the most iconic rooms is
the restaurant with the open sky roof
in summer.

Four Seasons
Florence, Italy

An old family palazzo, its proportions
are just wonderful. One of the biggest
private gardens...in the middle of Florence.
To me, that is luxury.

Alvear Palace Hotel
Buenos Aires, Argentina

Wonderful old charm.

Trianon Palace
Versailles, France

On the grounds of the most famous
château of all, Versailles. Go in the summer
and watch the fireworks and
listen to the orchestra (ideally, from
the balcony of your suite).

By the pool, 1968

The porch, 1969

OUR SCREENED-IN
PORCH—WHERE
MY PARENTS SAT AND
NEEDLEPOINTED
WHILE WE HUNG OUT
WITH OUR FRIENDS,
AFTER SWIMMING AND
PLAYING TENNIS.

OUR PORCH, BOTTOM
CENTER, WAS GREEN
AGAINST WHITE LATTICE
AND FRETWORK—
IT LOOKED LIKE A
BEAUTIFUL GRAPHIC
CHINTZ. FRETWORK
HAS SUBTLY INFLUENCED
OUR DESIGNS, FROM THE
COLLECTION TO THE
BRASS FRET CAP OF OUR
FRAGRANCE BOTTLE TO
THE BRASS BANISTERS
IN OUR BOUTIQUES.
IT'S A BRILLIANT, SIMPLE
DESIGN. CLOCKWISE
FROM TOP LEFT: ROMY
SCHNEIDER IN *LA PISCINE*,
1969; A SKETCH AND
A LOOK FROM SPRING
2014; A SISTER PARISH-
DESIGNED ROOM, BY
ARTHUR ELGORT, 2006;
BIRGITTA AF KLERCKER,
BY HORST P. HORST, 1965;
TWO LATTICE-INSPIRED
SPRING 2014 LOOKS.

OPEN, AIRY AND BRIGHT
SPACES IN DANIEL'S
HOME: TWO COLUMNS
PROTECT A SHEEP
BY FRANÇOIS-XAVIER
LALANNE (A FAVORITE
OF MINE); A BOLDLY
CONFIDENT BLACK
LACQUER LIBRARY.

DANIEL ROMUALDEZ ON ICONIC HOMES AND INTERIORS

The architect and interior designer's preferred color—none.

What inspires your work?
My clients—they all have different aesthetics. It's like being in university and taking different courses all the time. You don't get bored. I'm learning new things—period, furniture designers, artists…

What's your process?
It's like cooking. You say you like artichokes and eggplants. My job is to plan the menu, find the recipes, get it cooked right and serve you the meal that is all your favorite things.

Describe your personal style.
Minimal but…I'm curious.

Describe your space.
It's all off-white—I always wanted to have an all-white living room. And I have a black lacquer library.

Black lacquer is a statement…
It was inspired by Edwin Lutyens. When I was in school, I read that he had a black room because black is the combination of all colors. The spines of books and the Emilio Terry rug bring in lots of color.

Who else has influenced your work?
When I was growing up, it was Billy Baldwin, David Hicks and Cy Twombly. Later, there were the ladies who had beautiful houses: Marella Agnelli, Bunny Mellon and Lee Radziwill.

Time period aside, whose homes can't you forget?
The Villa Kérylos in the Côte d'Azur, in the south of France—the color palette, the severity, on the beach. That's heaven. Cy Twombly's apartment in Rome. Pauline de Rothschild's place in London. Villa Fiorentina.

How often do you change your rooms?
The art changes; the decor doesn't. Art reinvigorates a room. It shows different periods of my life. I just add (or subtract) things. The things that make me happy.

What do you love mixing the most?
People.

Let's free-associate.
Paint: white. **Prints:** plain. **Bedrooms:** cozy. **Living rooms:** comfortable. **Kitchens:** efficient. **Closets:** lots of room. **Color:** none.

MY BOYS AND ME,
BY NORMAN JEAN ROY
FOR *VOGUE*, 2012.

SETTING A TABLE CAN BE LIKE A DRAFTBOARD FOR DESIGNING—A PERFECT TIME FOR ME
TO EXPERIMENT WITH COLOR, PRINT AND INFLUENCES FROM ALL OVER.

LYNN WYATT ON ENTERTAINING

The consummate Texas hostess,
philanthropist and art patron's golden rules.

Have Fun

Once the first guest arrives, have fun
at your own party. It sets the tone.

Honor Someone

I like to have a guest of honor. I feel
fortunate that I've entertained dignitaries
and celebrities like Princess Grace of
Monaco, Gregory Peck, President Mikhail
Gorbachev and Mick Jagger. Having a guest
of honor gives a focus to the party.

Four Is the Magic Number

I usually have four courses: a soufflé,
vegetable terrine or wonderful, tasty soup;
osso buco or something en croute with
a great big crust in the winter (or in summer,
an herbal crusted fish with healthy veggies);
a salad and cheese course; then a yummy,
fattening dessert. If we started with
the bottom of the menu first, I'd love it.

Listen

Keep an open mind to other people's
opinions. As my husband, Oscar,
always says, "You can't learn anything with
your mouth open."

Be Polite

If one happens to be unhappy with one's
dinner companion, ask about his/her
viewpoint on a current subject to get him/
her talking. After all, it doesn't
have to be a meeting of the minds.
It's only dinner!

India, 2009

"Darkness settles on roofs and walls,
But the sea, the sea in the darkness calls…."
—HENRY WADSWORTH LONGFELLOW

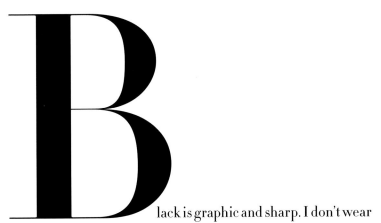

Black is graphic and sharp. I don't wear
it much, except maybe with navy—a combination that always seems to work. Black's power is nostalgic.
I love looking at Ron Galella's photos of celebrities in the Seventies, watching *The Philadelphia Story*
and the simple pleasure of reading the newspaper in bed. To this day, the single most important source of inspiration
behind our company comes from family albums filled with black-and-white photographs of my parents.

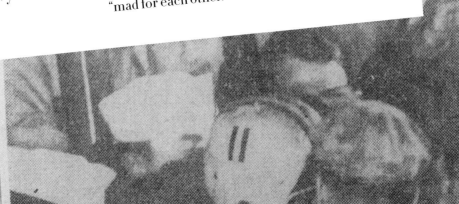

If I told you that I love you,
would you hold it against me?
LOVE, RELENTLESS

SOULMATE
I LOOK INTO YOUR EYES
AND SEE MY SOUL
WITHIN YOU
FILLED WITH LOVE

WHEN MY FATHER WAS COURTING MY MOTHER, HE WOULD SEND HER NOTES,
WHICH HE RAN IN THE NEWSPAPER'S WANTED SECTION.

Buddy & Reva

I can't think of a more romantic—or glamorous—couple than my parents, Buddy and Reva. Before they met each other, they had each had colorful love lives (Mom dated Steve McQueen; Dad stepped out once or twice with Grace Kelly). But when they met, they had instant chemistry—and they were everything to each other for the next 50 years.

In 1961, they jumped in my father's convertible BMW and eloped to Old Sturbridge Village, Massachusetts. They spent their honeymoon with champagne and sandwiches in a small New England hotel. They were never apart afterward.

They traveled—every summer, for six weeks, taking a big steamer ship to Italy, France, Greece and Morocco. They celebrated an official honeymoon at La Mamounia in Marrakech, and kept going back every few years. And every single day they were, in my mother's words, "mad for each other."

STATES—FOUNDED 1771

𝕴𝖓𝖖𝖚𝖎𝖗𝖊𝖗

FINAL
CITY EDITION

L THE

963
No. 58

Athens, Early 1970s

Southampton

MARRAKECH

Growing up, I loved hearing my parents talk about their time at La Mamounia, in Marrakech. They would walk around the markets and souks, picking up spices, fabrics and antiques.

Years later, Morocco lived up to my imagination—the charm of the culture, the architecture and the mountains, the tapestries, tilework and food. It's fascinating that Alfred Hitchcock set *The Man Who Knew Too Much* there. Or, as legend has it, was inspired to write *The Birds*. It must be true—I heard the crows every morning.

Marrakech is a great starting point for design inspiration. There is Yves Saint Laurent's Majorelle Garden, surrounded by its distinct saturated blue; the souks with their fragrant spice stalls; the alleyways hiding beautiful architecture and details that have been there for centuries.

Family — where it all begins for me...

Sawyer, Montana, 2005

Nicholas & me, Hawaii, 2013

With the boys and Chris, 2002

Izzie, Pookie, Louisa & me, New York City, 1998

Henry, Sawyer & Nick, Southampton, 2012

EVERYONE IN OUR FAMILY HAS A NICKNAME. MY BOYS ARE CALLED SAUCY, HANKY AND PICKLE.
THE GIRLS ARE IZZIE, POOKIE AND WHEEZY. GROWING UP, I WAS TOAD (NOT MY CHOICE).

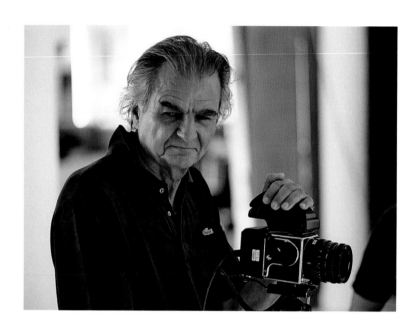

PATRICK DEMARCHELIER
ON HIS FAVORITE SUBJECTS

The famed fashion photographer talks about cameras, curiosity and color.

What is your first memory of photographs?
My first camera was my eye. I was very curious when
I was young, and I looked at everything. Even now,
my eye is my camera.

When is a photograph perfect?
I like spontaneity. I like the moment. I like people
to be themselves and to express themselves in some
way. To catch them off guard.

Photographers and artists who inspire you...
When I was young, I liked Irving Penn.

Best piece of advice you have ever received...
You have to always work very hard. Every day
is a new job and challenge.

Whom do you love to shoot the most?
I like everything. I like animals better—they
don't pose for the camera because they don't
know what it is. The best subject was my dog.
It was my best portrait.

**In your opinion, the most important photo you
have ever taken...**
The one I'm taking tomorrow. The next one.

Do you prefer shooting in color or black and white?
Black and white.

What's your favorite color?
I like blue. Dark blue. I don't know why.
I just like dark blue.

EVERYTHING IN MY HOME
HAS A MEMORY TIED TO
IT. EVERY ROOM STARTS
WITH IDEAS THAT
REPRESENT DIFFERENT
TIMES AND PLACES IN
MY LIFE—FROM MY PARENTS'
HOME, PRESENTS FROM
FRIENDS AND THINGS
I FIND ON TRIPS, AT
AUCTIONS OR IN LOCAL
MARKETS. WHEN WE
FIRST MOVED INTO OUR
HOME IN SOUTHAMPTON,
IT WAS SPARE, AND WHITE.
DANIEL ROMUALDEZ, WHO
WAS WORKING WITH ME ON
THE RENOVATION, LOVED
THE BLACK-AND-WHITE
CHECKERED FLOORS,
PHOTOGRAPHED HERE
BY FRANÇOIS HALARD. THEY
REMINDED HIM OF A STRIKING
HALLWAY DESIGNED BY
THE GREAT BRITISH
ARCHITECT EDWIN LUTYENS,
HIS INSPIRATION.

AN IDEA FOR A COLLECTION
CAN COME FROM
ANYWHERE. CLOCKWISE
FROM NEAR RIGHT: CECIL
BEATON'S SELF-PORTRAIT;
ME, STANDING IN RANDOM
INTERNATIONAL'S *RAIN
ROOM*, AT THE MUSEUM OF
MODERN ART, 2013; EDIE
SEDGWICK AND ANDY
WARHOL BY UGO MULAS,
1954 (© 2014 THE ANDY
WARHOL FOUNDATION FOR
THE VISUAL ARTS, INC./
ARTISTS RIGHTS SOCIETY
[ARS], NEW YORK); PABLO
PICASSO BY ROBERT
DOISNEAU, 1952 (PABLO
PICASSO © 2014 ESTATE OF
PICASSO/ARTISTS RIGHTS
SOCIETY [ARS], NEW YORK);
STEPHEN SUMNER'S *WHITE
NOISE*, 2013; JASPER
JOHNS'S *JUBILEE*, 1959,
AND, AT CENTER, LOUISE
BOURGEOIS'S *MAMAN*, 1999.

"AS KARL
LAGERFELD SAID,
'BLACK, LIKE
WHITE, IS THE BEST
COLOR.' THEY'RE
MY FAVORITES, TOO,
PLUS A TOUCH
OF GRAY. THEY CAN
BE DRAMATIC BUT
EVOKE MYSTERY
AND EMOTION,
LIKE STEPHEN
SUMNER'S PAINTING
WHITE NOISE."

—GLENDA BAILEY,
ON SUMNER'S *WHITE NOISE*

A BEAUTIFUL, CURVING, FEMININE FLORAL CAN BE JUST AS POWERFUL
AS A STRONG GRAPHIC. LOOKS FROM FALL 2013 AND MY COLLECTION
OF WHITE PORCELAIN VEGETABLES I FOUND IN PARIS.

FROM LEFT, TOP ROW: WITH PERRI PELTZ, DINA POWELL, TAMARA MELLEN, KITTY SHERRILL, JAMIE ALEXANDER TISCH, GIGI MORTIMER, STEPHANIE VON WATZDORF; LINDA LEE WITH HER DAUGHTERS LUCY AND ZOEY YOON; FIONA KOTUR; CRYSTAL LOURD AND JAMIE; WITH OPRAH WINFREY; LYNN WYATT. SECOND ROW: POOKIE WITH MARIO GRAUSO AND SERKAN SARIER; LOUISA GENT; JESSICA ALBA AND CASH WARREN; WITH LAZARO HERNANDEZ, JACK MCCOLLOUGH AND NARCISO RODRIGUEZ; WITH TREY LAIRD AND HONOR BRODIE; ANNA WINTOUR. THIRD ROW: CAROLINE GUTHRIE AND KERRY-LYNNE CARRERA; LILLIAN WANG VON STAUFFENBERG; ALICE TISCH (WALKING); ROS L'ESPERANCE; WITH SUSAN BURCH AND SAWYER; LILLIAN AND KAREN GROOS AND THEIR CHILDREN; NANDINI D'SOUZA WOLFE; WITH EVE HOOD. FOURTH ROW: SAMANTHA GREGORY; DENISE ROME; MICHELLE DURHAM; WITH CARLOS MOTA AND RENEE ROCKEFELLER; GIGI, ELIZABETH LINDEMANN AND DANIELLE GANEK; BROOKLYN DECKER AND LIYA KEBEDE; AERIN LAUDER.

Porto Ercole, 2008

"The fountains mingle with the river
And the rivers with the ocean,
The winds of heaven mix for ever
With a sweet emotion."
—PERCY BYSSHE SHELLEY

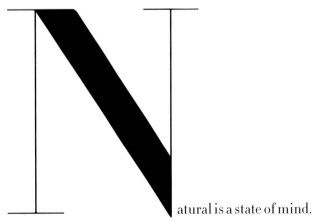

Natural is a state of mind.
Being in nature inspires me, whether I'm walking on the beach, fishing with my boys or exploring
ruins in an ancient city. So much of this inspiration finds its way into our textures, prints
and fabrics. And I always find women to be the most beautiful when they're natural and undone.

MY MOTHER'S SIGNATURE IS LEOPARD. MAYBE IT STARTED HERE—1950S CUBA, AT THE HABANA RIVIERA HOTEL, OPPOSITE, WHEN THEY ASKED HER TO SIT FOR THIS PHOTOGRAPH. THIS PICTURE ALWAYS HANGS ON OUR OFFICE WALL.

Jamaica, 1970

At my summer camp, 1972

Majorca, 1960

REVA

It's hard to put in a few pages—I would need volumes—what I've learned from my mother or what she means to me. Perhaps one of the most profound decisions she ever made was to move our family to the end of the Main Line and into the country. Where, every morning after breakfast, she opened the door and let us be outside until dinner. Usually, she was outside, too, in her garden.

She is many things: consummate entertainer and hostess, perfectionist, homework warden, optimist, athlete and artist. Everyone was welcome in our home. She would throw big parties—for which she did all the decor. Yet the same care and attention was given to family dinners on a school night.

She instilled in all of us the idea that the glass is half full, which my brothers and I hope we've passed on to our children. She often says, "You are as happy as your least happy child."

And she is one of the most stylish women I know. She loves great design, from architecture to fashion. Growing up, I remember spending hours in her closet among the rows of meticulously kept Yves Saint Laurent, Halston, Norman Norell, Christian Dior, Jean Patou… She bought me my first dress, a black tulle Saint Laurent gown with pink sequins for my high school prom. And she introduced me to Zoran, one of her favorite designers, who eventually gave me my first job in fashion in New York.

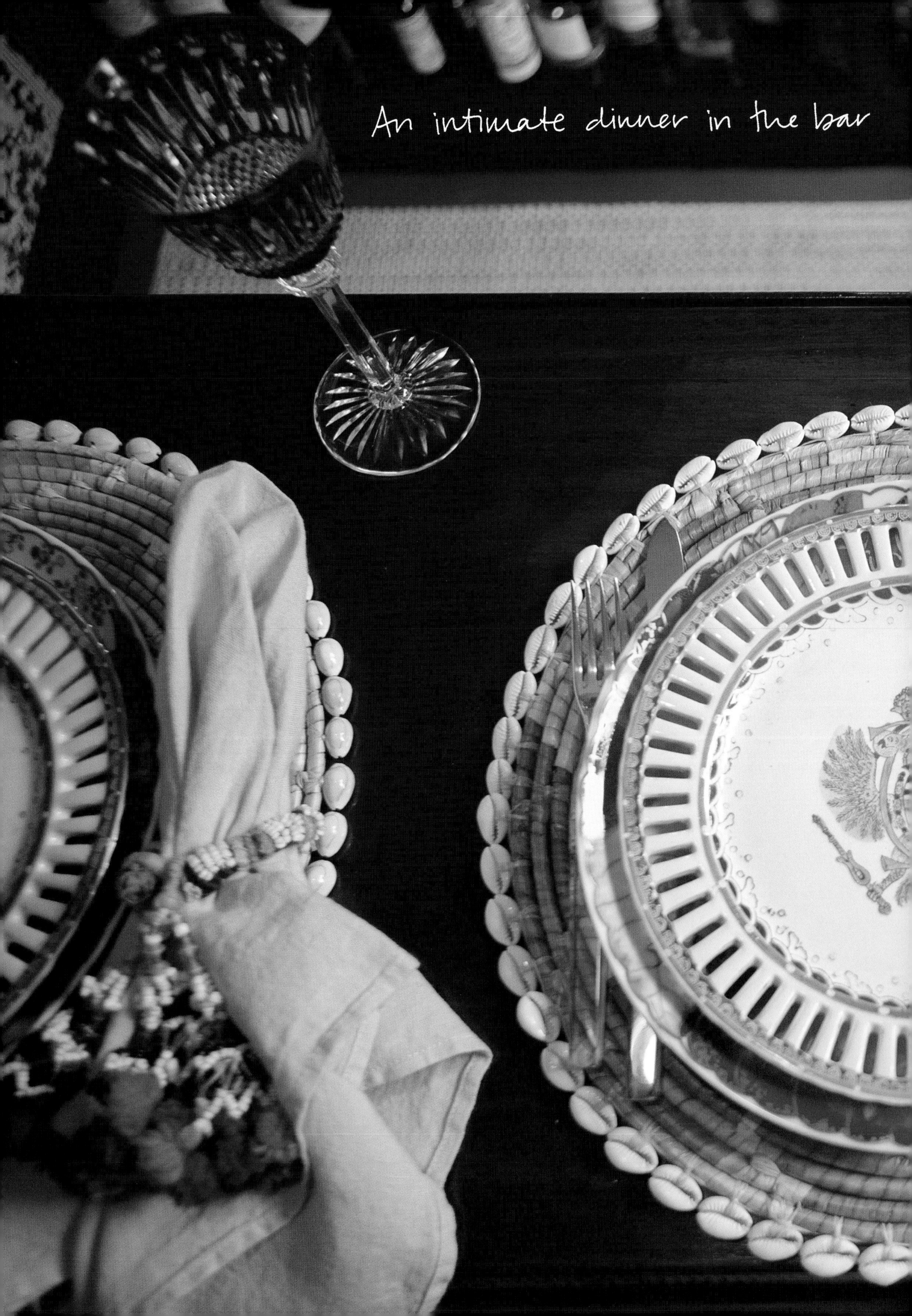

An intimate dinner in the bar

LEOPARD

Leopard is classic, in fashion and at home.
Two Billy Baldwin poufs in my living
room draw attention to a table of family
photos, rock crystal lamps and, at the
center, Tom Wesselmann's *Study for Great
American Nude, #68*, 1966; cheeky pillows
my parents needlepointed that I keep in my
office and home; and a perfect vintage coat.

With Louisa and Pookie, Milan, 2010

SAWYER, LEFT, RIDES
BY WALTON FORD'S *SO
PANTETH MY SOUL
AFTER THEE*, 2001, IN
OUR APARTMENT; BY
FRANÇOIS HALARD, 2004.

Walton Ford, Algiers Point, 2013

DEEDA BLAIR ON
BEAUTIFUL ROOMS

An essay from the elegant champion of medical research.

I think the key to rooms is very good architecture, as it has an influence on the way life is lived. Years ago, I received advice from Billy Baldwin, who firmly said, "You should plan what is going to happen in the entire room, beginning with the all-important floor plan for the furniture. Colors, fabrics, wall treatments and the addition of both the necessary and the unexpected come later."

The most interesting and successful rooms do not look as if a decorator arrived and did everything. Rooms should reflect the people who live in them, their lives and what inspires them. It could be the colors in porcelain or a collection of paintings—the frequently chalky paint of Louis XVI chairs or black lacquer table desks.

Beautiful rooms are seldom haphazard. Because something is inherited does not mean it has to be kept. Be ruthless—give away or sell what you don't love.

Add your own approach to achieve something unusual. It is nice to be able to make subtle changes in atmosphere by switching a few things periodically— like a tablecloth or pillows.

Different flowers and carefully selected containers can transform a room. A lovely bouquet at the entrance can be wonderful; however, for most rooms I am of the less-is-more view—I love the individual beauty of a single rose, peony or delphinium, a small cluster of hyacinths, maidenhair ferns and jasmine plants.

Most important is atmosphere. I feel it is important to leave space, and a feeling of air and light, and to use living things—plants, trees, flowers. The decoration should not be overemphasized. It is not meant to be a display, but rather about what is personal—and loved by the owner.

My boys, Bali, 2009
My screen saver for years...

With Mercedes Castillo and Stephanie, 2012

STEPHANIE VON WATZDORF
ON THE BEST
MARKETS & BAZAARS

The Creative Director and Founder of Figue knows
where to go for the unexpected find.

Brimfield
Massachusetts

The Rose Bowl
Los Angeles

The Grand Bazaar
Istanbul

Souk Semmarine
Marrakech

Chor Bazaar
Mumbai

Saturday Night Market
Goa

Dilli Haat
New Delhi

Porte de Clignancourt
Paris

Portobello Road
London

Maasai Market
Nairobi

I LOVE TEXTURES:
THE STUCCO FACADE,
STONE WALLS AND RELIEFS
OF OUR VALLEY FORGE
HOME OR OLD CITIES;
THE BURLAP TABLE LINENS
MY MOTHER MADE FOR BIG
PARTIES; THE SISAL RUGS
I HAVE IN NEARLY EVERY
ROOM OF MY HOME;
THE RAFFIA, EMBROIDERY,
BEADS AND APPLIQUÉS
IN OUR COLLECTION, LIKE
SPRING 2013, RIGHT.

The sunroom, Southampton

Paris, 2010

Rome, 2011

London, 2010

JORDAN SALCITO & ROBERT BOHR
ON WINE

The couple—both sommeliers
and entrepreneurs—talk about best bottles,
labels and prisms of color.

Best region for falling in love...
Burgundy.

Most beautiful bottle and label...
Maximin Grünhauser Abtsberg,
Carl Von Schubert, Ruwer, Mosel, Germany.

The best wine lists...
Saison and RN74 in San Francisco;
The French Laundry in Yountville, CA;
Eleven Madison Park in New York.
Maison Troisgros, in Roanne, France;
Almhof Schneider, in Lech, Austria.

Bottle you always give...
If it's a special birthday, we like to give "birth
year" wines. For all other occasions, champagne.

What about the color of wine?
The color of great wine is described by its
brilliance, like a rare gemstone.
A great wine's brilliance may contain rubies,
diamonds and emeralds. Light in a
great wine will refract into a prism of colors
that dance in the glass's reflection.

India, 2009

"Nature's first green is gold,
Her hardest hue to hold.
Her early leaf's a flower;
But only so an hour."
—ROBERT FROST

G

old—warm, personal, glamorous.
I gravitate towards it. It's my signature: I always wear a ring, necklace or cuff. Years before I would
wear my first dress and decades before our gold logo was designed, I had an object lesson
in the power of gold: I was five or six, sitting in my mom's closet watching her get ready to go out.
She threw on a gold lamé top and skirt by Zoran. *Divine.*

A TABLE BY YVES KLEIN—
HE WAS INSPIRED
BY GOLD BUDDHAS IN
JAPAN IN THE EARLY
1950S. I LIKE THE MIX
OF DIFFERENT ELEMENTS
IN THIS TABLE—GOLD
AGAINST GREEN-AND-
WHITE PARROT TULIPS OR
A DECONSTRUCTED
CLASSICAL VASE BY ARTIST
FRANCESCA DIMATTIO.

The Night Before Christmas...

We covered our Christmas tree with
tinsel, ornaments and snow. And at the end,
my mom carefully put the angel on top.
We drank hot chocolate and put out cookies
and milk for Santa before going to bed.
We would pile into one room and tell ghost
stories. Meanwhile, my parents would
stay up for hours setting up toy trains,
dollhouses, and who knows what else,
so that the next morning, the room was like
a winter wonderland. Wrapping was my
favorite thing to do—next to playing jokes
on my brothers. One year, I wrapped
kitchen utensils, bricks and anything random
I could find and put them under my
brother Jamie's pile. He wasn't amused.

SEVENTIES SPORTSWEAR

I have always loved the Seventies—Yves Saint Laurent at the pinnacle of his genius and icons like Marisa Berenson, Julie Christie and Jacqueline Kennedy Onassis. It was the era when designers like Geoffrey Beene, Bill Blass and Halston were defining classic American sportswear. Amy Fine Collins, a *Vanity Fair* writer and author, says it perfectly: "Seventies sportswear represented the triumph of the funky boutique over the couture salon, the victory of American freedom over Continental tradition. It was about pride in the body and how it moved."

The 1970s was when my mom discovered Zoran, an eccentric designer from Croatia. I vividly remember her getting ready to go out in her lamé top and pants—there was nothing so glamorous. Years later, we referenced that glittering moment for Spring 2011, albeit pairing lamé back to a baja pullover. And when we profiled Anna Dello Russo, above left, on ur blog, she showed us all how lamé is always, always of-the-moment. Amy agrees: "Gold lamé is forever—it is as flattering as candlelight and as mood-elevating as dancing."

GOLD JEWELRY

Jewelry has always been a part of my style.
While I like bold pieces, most of what I wear
is also sentimental: my father's Zippo-pendant,
my mother's Greek cuffs or a horn necklace
(above), given to me by Fiona Kotur. My high
school friend Kara Ross, the designer
and gemologist, shares my love of jewelry—
costume and fine. She has been interested
in gems since she was 15. "Interesting designs
can make the stones seem even more
magical," she says. "I feel the strongest about
jewelry that I acquired or created during the
milestones of my life—they constantly remind
me of those moments."

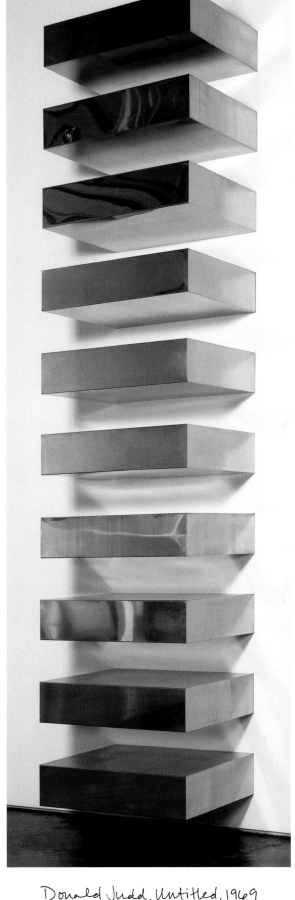

Donald Judd, Untitled, 1969

DONALD JUDD'S
STACKS, RIGHT, INTRUDE
INTO A ROOM, BOLD
AND GLAMOROUS
(THOUGH JUDD WOULD
HAVE REJECTED
THAT WORD OUTRIGHT).

―――――――

"LESS IS MORE."
A GREAT EXAMPLE?
THIS PHOTOGRAPH
OF MY MOTHER
IN THE EARLY 1970S.

Irving Penn, Ginkgo Leaves, New York, 1990

WHEAT

Wheat, a print in our Spring 2013 collection, is eternally optimistic. It is an ancient symbol of rebirth through the earth, of going from the dark to the light. It is life-giving and revered in nearly every culture.

Demeter, the goddess of the harvest, gave the Greeks and Romans wheat, while the Egyptians buried their dead with sheaves of wheat, food for the journey through the afterlife. Vincent van Gogh, who obsessively painted wheat fields, wrote to his sister, "What the germinating force is to the grain, love is to us."

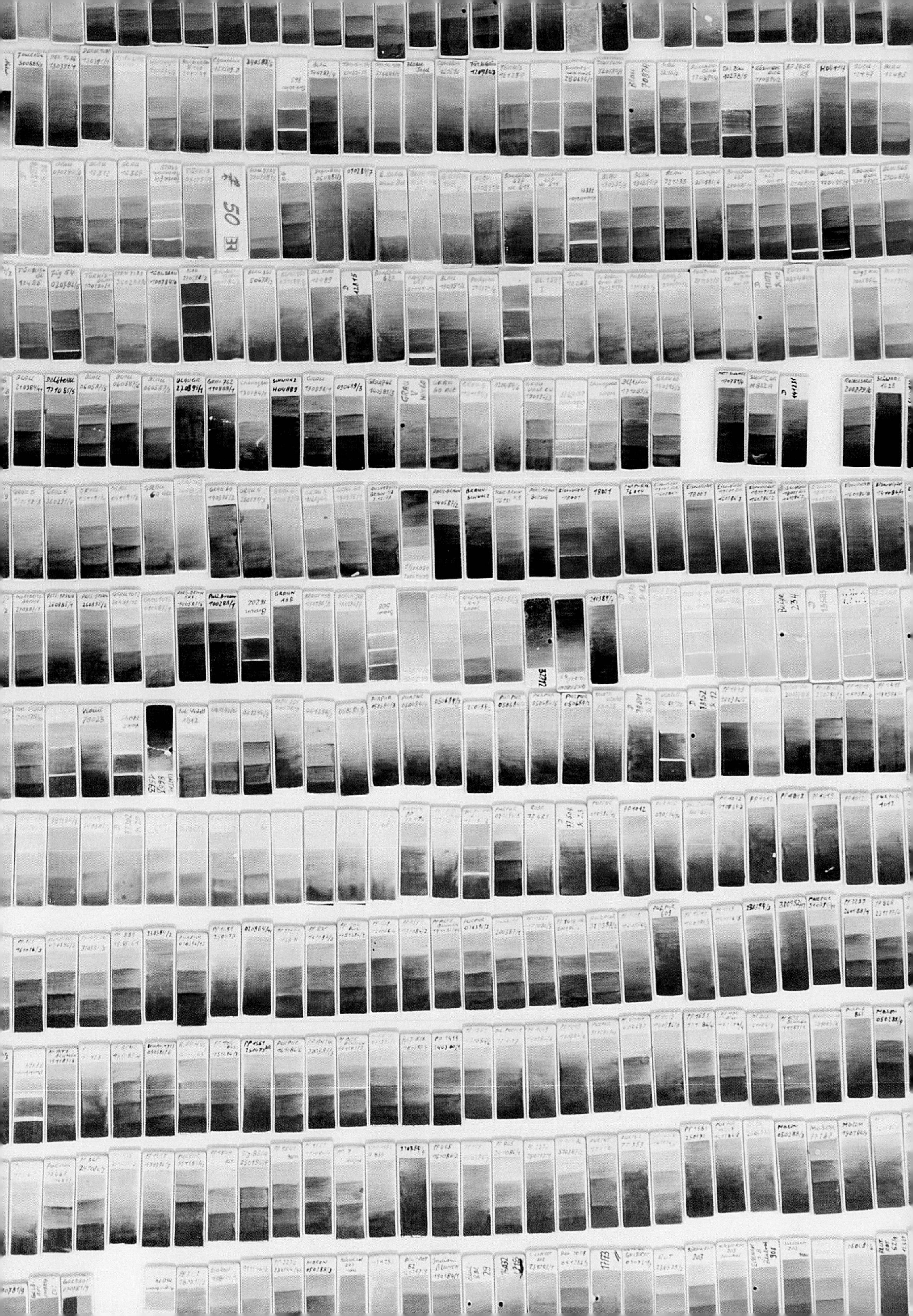

DR. SAMANTHA BOARDMAN ON THE SCIENCE OF COLOR

Another way of looking at orange, blue, green, purple, pink…

What is the relation of science and color?

The influence of color on behavior and psychological process is well documented. Psychologist Ulrich Beer captures our visceral response perfectly: "No one can encounter it and stay neutral. We are immediately, instinctively and emotionally moved. We have sympathy or antipathy, pleasure or disapproval, within us as soon as we perceive colors."

Do the colors we wear affect our mood or how others treat us?

One of the first things we notice about someone is the color of what they are wearing. It shapes the way others see us as well as how we see ourselves. Waitresses wearing red lipstick receive bigger tips, and studies show men find women in red clothing to be more attractive, more sexually desirable, and they tend to sit closer to them. Ladies wearing red tend to feel more attractive—they stand taller, smile more radiantly and are more outgoing.

Can it have a negative effect?

Hockey players who wear black uniforms are penalized more often than players in other colors. The question is whether referees perceive them as more aggressive and penalize them accordingly or whether players feel more aggressive in black uniforms.

Does pink really make a person nicer, gentler?

In the book *Drunk Tank Pink*, Adam Alter describes how a certain shade of pink decreases aggression among prisoners and improves behavior. The University of Iowa's locker room for visiting football teams is famously painted pink for the exact same reason— to calm opponents and put them in a passive mood.

Any other interesting associations?

Color is especially powerful when it comes to food. The exact same wine was rated higher when drunk in a room with ambient red or blue light rather than green or white light. The color of the glass may alter the taste of wine, while plate color has been shown to influence flavor. People prefer strawberry mousse served on a white plate to the identical mousse served on a black one.

What's your personal take on the science of color?

It helps us navigate the world around us. Conventions, expectations and associations influence the way we experience color—a bride in black or a widow in fuchsia is deemed inappropriate; attending a funeral in gold sequins would be disrespectful. It isculturally embedded, intensely personal and yet has a mind of its own. As Van Gogh said, "Color expresses something by itself."

FROM TOP: OUR LEADERSHIP TEAM, IN 2013; MEMBERS OF OUR EXECUTIVE, DESIGN, CREATIVE, MARKETING AND STORES TEAMS STANDING IN FRONT OF OUR SOON-TO-OPEN MADISON AVENUE BOUTIQUE—COVERED IN AN ILLUSTRATION WE DID WITH THE ARTIST JAMES DE LA VEGA IN 2011.

ACKNOWLEDGMENTS

My mother once said Tory Burch isn't a company; it's a family. As we close this book,
we are a team of 2,500. I am grateful for each and every person's passion and dedication.
Everyone is vital in telling our story, whether it's by welcoming visitors to a boutique,
writing an email subject line, getting a pair of shoes ready to ship or sketching
ideas that will, ultimately, end up on the runway. Thank you.

A special thanks to my friends and family who supported us while we created this book.
To Nicholas, Henry, Sawyer, Pookie, Louisa, Izzie, Mom, Robert and Patty,
Jamie and Nicole, Leonard and Erika, Julie Ragoo, Alma Dionisio, Chris Calabrese,
Paul Hurtado, Bill Allen, Angela Lopez and Madison Sheldon.

For their incredible insight, a special thank you to Jeanne Greenberg Rohatyn
and her team at Salon 94; to Larry Gagosian and Chrissie Erpf, and the Gagosian Gallery;
to Daniel Romualdez.

Thank you to Ashley Hicks for graciously giving us access to his family's archive.
To The Barnes Foundation and the Condé Nast Archives.

To our colleagues Rebecca Kaplan and John Gall at Abrams,
and Jennifer Rudolph Walsh and Andy McNicol at WME.

To the book team: Honor Brodie, Nandini D'Souza Wolfe, Emily Wardwell,
Ally Lewis, Louisa Gent, Noa Griffel, Suki Wong, Sasha Tulchin,
Alexa Elam and Larsen McDowell.

To all those—and many more—who helped the book team
(in alphabetical order): Adam Ben'Ous, Miki Berardelli, Dana Buselt, Berta Camal,
Kerry-Lynne Carrera, Amber Case, Monica Cuellar, Louise Denny, Tina Dunn,
Kate Etter, Hadley Garrettson, Jessica Gillan, Gina Grant, Caroline Guthrie, Dasha Kuni,
Fiana Kwasnik, Venessa Lau, Alice Luo, Abby Lynn, Erin Mazzoni, Fiona Meehan, Ashley
Middleton, Dana Minuta, Kristi Morse, Dan Palmer, Frances Pennington, Lauren Picker,
Michael Ray, Amanda Sachs, Reepal Shah, Esther Song, Sarah Stark, Whitney Tressel,
Lindsay Wallner, Annie Weiss, Kellie Yuan and all our incredible interns.

The design team, Post-show, September 2013

Carmen Almon, Plumbago, 2014

"GIVING SOMEONE PURPLE FLOWERS CAN CHANGE
THEIR LUCK FOR THE BETTER. PURPLE IS
RARE IN NATURE—FINDING IT IS A GOOD SIGN."

— MR. SIU

MONA WU, WHO HAS BEEN WITH US SINCE THE BEGINNING IN OUR HONG KONG OFFICE,
WOULDN'T WORK WITH US UNTIL I CONSULTED A FENG SHUI MASTER. IN 2006,
OUR NEW YORK COLLEAGUE CINDY TRAN INTRODUCED US TO MR. SIU, WHO HAS BEEN GUIDING US WISELY EVER
SINCE. WHENEVER HE IS IN THE OFFICE, PEOPLE LINE UP FOR ADVICE—ABOUT WORK, LOVE, LIFE.

I have music playing all day—at home,
in the car, at work, at parties.
One last playlist, from my longtime friend
Marjorie Gubelmann, aka DJ Mad Marj...

Rumors Timex Social Club

West End Girls Pet Shop Boys

Beat Goes On Madonna ft. Kanye West

Could You Be Loved Bob Marley

Rock the Casbah The Clash

In da Club 50 Cent

Nobody's Diary Yaz

Hey Nineteen Steeley Dan

Hot-n-Fun NERD ft. Nelly Furtado

La Vie en Rose Grace Jones

Close to Me The Cure

I Melt With You Modern English

Just Got Paid Johnny Kemp

Gimme Gimme Gimme Abba

Family Affair Mary J. Blige

CREDITS

Cover and Title Page
Beautiful Primal Urges Rug 100% wool, 130 knots per square inch, handwoven 3000 mm (diameter) © Damien Hirst and Science Ltd. All rights reserved. DACS, London/ARS, NY 2014. Courtesy of Other Criteria.

Page 8 François Halard/Trunk Archive.

Pages 10-11 Martien Mulder/Trunk Archive.

Page 12 Norman Jean Roy/Trunk Archive.

Page 13 "Caged Bird" from *Shaker, Why Don't You Sing?* by Maya Angelou, copyright © 1983 by Maya Angelou. Used by permission of Random House, an imprint and division of Random House LLC and Virago, an imprint of Little, Brown Book Group UK. All rights reserved. Third-party use requires permission from Random House LLC.

Page 14 © The Estate of David Hicks.

Page 15 François Halard/Trunk Archive.

Page 16 Tory © Jeffrey Prehn.

Page 21 Cast-bronze *Tear Drop*, 2006, & *Wishbone*, 2002, by Charles Price. *An Indian Album* by Cecil Beaton © Batsford 1945.

Pages 22-23 Mark Rothko, *Orange and Red on Red*, 1957, oil on canvas © 1998 Kate Rothko Prizel & Christopher Rothko, The Phillips Collection, Washington, DC. Interior: Horst/*House & Garden*; © Condé Nast. From left: Franz Kline © 2014 The Franz Kline Estate; Willem de Kooning © 2014 The Willem de Kooning Foundation; Rothko © 1998 Kate Rothko Prizel & Christopher Rothko. All credited artworks: Artists Rights Society (ARS), New York.

Page 24 Painting in dining room: Franco Gentilini, © 2014 Artists Rights Society (ARS), New York/SIAE, Rome. Wrap bracelets, Holly Tote & Robinson wallets & clutches: Ilan Rubin/Trunk Archive. Menu: La Grenouille. Romy Schneider: Photononstop/Superstock. Quilted Fleming Bag: Angelo Pennetta/Trunk Archive. Runway: Dan & Corina Lecca; stylist: Tabitha Simmons/Streeters; models: Frida Aasen & Sasha Luss/Women Management.

Page 25 Stylist: Tabitha Simmons/Streeters; Model: Anais Mali/DNA Model Management.

Page 27 Recipe: Dana Minuta.

Pages 28-29 Twins: Pookie Burch.

Page 30 Sawyer: Pookie Burch.

Page 33 Tory, left: Mimi Ritzen Crawford. Models: Jennifer Livingston/Trunk Archive. Bari Mattes: Anthony Alvarez.

Page 35 W. S. Merwin, excerpt from "The Sapphire" from *The First Four Books of Poems.* Copyright © 1956, 2000 by W. S. Merwin. Reprinted with the permission of The Permissions Company, Inc., on behalf of Copper Canyon Press, www.coppercanyon-press.org, and by The Wylie Agency, LLC.

Page 37 Harmony Korine, *Blue Checker*, 2014; oil on canvas, 102 x 84 in. (259.1 x 213.4 cm); © Harmony Korine. Courtesy of Gagosian Gallery. Photograph: Robert McKeever.

Page 38 Paul Costello. Arbre de Matisse Reverse wall covering & upholstery from Quadrille/China Seas.

Page 39 Painting: *Perfect Sleeper*, 2002 © Cameron Martin.

Pages 40-41 Topkapi Palace: Simon Watson/Trunk Archive. Tory: Norman Jean Roy/Trunk Archive, originally for *Vogue.*

Pages 44-45 Tunic: Jonny Valiant. Tory: Norman Jean Roy/Trunk Archive.

Pages 46-47 Clockwise from top left: Spring 2013 runway: Dan & Corina Lecca; stylist: Tabitha Simmons/Streeters; model: Katlin Aas/IMG Models. Grace Kelly: © Bettmann/Corbis. Jean Shrimpton: Lichfield/*Vogue*; © Condé Nast. Prince: Photo by Dove Shore/Getty Images. Ali MacGraw: Richardson/*Mademoiselle*; © Condé Nast. Summer 2014: Angelo Pennetta/Trunk Archive; stylist: Ethel Park; models: Bette Franke/DNA Model Management, Frida Aasen/Women Management, Caroline Brasch Nielsen/The Society Management. Kenneth Jay Lane: Fairchild Photo Service.

Page 48 Norman Jean Roy/Trunk Archive; stylist: Brian Molloy/Tim Howard Management; model: Shu Pei/Next Model Management.

Page 49 Tory: Gordon Hull/Tory Burch LLC. Artisan: There Is No Limit Foundation.

Pages 50-51 Fabric: Jonny Valiant. Armor: Gordon Hull/Tory Burch LLC.

Page 52 Richard Diebenkorn (American, 1922–1993), *Ocean Park No. 68*, 1974, oil on canvas, 81 x 95 in. (205.74 x 236.22 cm), Milwaukee Art Museum, Gift of Jane Bradley Pettit MI980.183. Photo: John R. Glembin. © The Richard Diebenkorn Foundation.

Page 54 *Hawaii* by James A. Michener, 1959 Edition; Random House LLC.

Page 56 "Ithaka," translated by Edmund Keeley; copyright © C. P. Cavafy; © 1975 & 1992 by Edmund Keeley and Philip Sherrard. Reprinted by permission of Princeton University Press and The Estate of C. P. Cavafy c/o Rogers, Coleridge & White Ltd., 20 Powis Mews, London W11 1JN.

Page 58 Column 1: Gloria Guinness: Beaton/*Vogue*; © Condé Nast. Spring 2012: Stylist: Brian Molloy/Tim Howard Management; model: Anna Selezneva/Women Management. Beach: © Bettmann/Corbis. Models in stripes: Penati/*Vogue*; © Condé Nast. Column 2: Resort 2014: Angelo Pennetta/Trunk Archive; stylist: Ethel Park; models: Laura Kampman/New York Model Management & Mirte Maas/Women Management. Book cover: *The Colossus of Maroussi* by Henry Miller, © 1941 Henry Miller; reprinted by permission of New Directions Corp. Truman Capote: Fairchild Photo Service. Bibi Cornejo Borthwick: Hanuk. Column 3: Bicycle: Demarchelier/*Vogue*; © Condé Nast. Swing: Stephanie Gonot. Marina Rust & Ian Connor: Courtesy of Marina Rust. Bonnie Morrison and Ally Lewis (Column 4, top): photographed for *The Tory Blog*. Swimmer: Horst/*Vogue*; © Condé Nast (bottom). Column 5: Elizabeth Olsen: Angelo Pennetta/Trunk Archive. Koos collection: Fairchild Photo Service.

Page 59 Stylist: Brian Molloy/Tim Howard Management; model: Anna Selezneva/Women Management.

Page 60 Norman Jean Roy/Trunk Archive.

Pages 64-65 Photo: Tina Barney; stylist: Samira Nasr/Management + Artists; models: Madison Malerba/Generation; Trish Goff/DNA Model Management; Polly Mellen; Noot Seear/One Management.

Page 66 Interior: Kertész/*House & Garden*; © Condé Nast. Hubert de Givenchy: Kai Jünemann.

Page 67 Faust/*Architectural Digest*; © Condé Nast.

Pages 68-69 Clockwise from top left: Marisa Berenson: Slim Aarons/Premium Archive/Getty Images. Book cover from *One Hundred Years of Solitude* by Gabriel García Márquez, translated by Gregory Rabassa. English translation copyright © 1970 by Harper & Row Publishers, Inc. Reprinted by permission of HarperCollins Publishers. Hanneli Mustaparta: Marko MacPherson. Cover reprinted with permission of Scribner Publishing Group, a division of Simon & Schuster, Inc. from *Tender Is the Night* by F. Scott Fitzgerald. Copyright © (New York, 1934). All rights reserved. Sawyer's letter: Jonny Valiant.

Page 71 François Halard/Trunk Archive.

Pages 72-73 Tabitha Simmons: Matteo Prandoni/BFAnyc.com. Fall 2013: Dan & Corina Lecca; stylist: Tabitha Simmons/Streeters; model: Bette Franke/DNA Model Management.

Page 75 Dodie Thayer courtesy of Dodie Thayer.

Page 77 Ellsworth Kelly, *Wild Grape*, 1961, watercolor, 22.5 x 28.5 in. (57.2 x 72.4 cm) © Ellsworth Kelly.

Page 78 Kovarsky/*The New Yorker*; © Condé Nast.

Page 81 Recipe: Dana Minuta.

Page 82 Angelo Pennetta/Trunk Archive; stylist: Ethel Park; model: Bette Franke/DNA Model Management.

Page 83 Runway: Dan & Corina Lecca; stylist: Tabitha Simmons/Streeters; models: Anna Ewers, Fei Fei Sun, Frida Aasen, Sam Rollinson/Women Management; Anais Mali & Ondria Hardin/DNA Model Management; Janice Alida/Elite NYC; Diana Moldovan, Tilda Lindstam, Yumi Lambert/IMG Models; Holly Rose Emery/Next Model Management; Ashleigh Good/Ford Models; Nadja Bender/New York Model Management.

Page 87 Elgort/*Vogue*; © Condé Nast.

Page 91 Garden plan: Perry Guillot, Landscape Architect.

Page 92 Angelo Pennetta/Trunk Archive; stylist: Ethel Park; model: Laura Kampman/New York Model Management.

Page 93 Richard Prince, *Untitled* (jokes), 2006; acrylic on canvas, 78 x 66 in. (198.1 x 167.6 cm); © Richard Prince. Courtesy of Gagosian Gallery. Photograph: Robert McKeever.

Page 100 Top row, left: Tory with *Smooth Egg with Bow* (Blue/Magenta), 1994–2009; mirror-polished stainless steel with transparent color coating; 83.5 x 76.625 x 62 in.; 212.1 x 194.6 x 157.5 cm © Jeff Koons. Marisa Berenson: Slim Aarons/Premium Archive/Getty Images. Bottom row, left: *Redbud*: Leanne Shapton, from *The Native Trees of Canada*, Drawn & Quarterly 2010.

Page 101 *Hanging Heart (Violet/Gold)*, 1994–2006; mirror-polished stainless steel with transparent color coating; 114.625 x 110.25 x 40 inches; 291 x 280 x 101.5 cm © Jeff Koons. Photograph: Sandy Volz.

Pages 102-103 © Noa Griffel, 2010.

Page 105 Joe Schildhorn/BFAnyc.com.

Page 106 © X17 Agency.

Page 108 Lucio Fontana, *Concetto Spaziale, Attese* © 2014 Artists Rights Society (ARS), New York/SIAE, Rome. Photo © Christie's Images Limited 2010.

Pages 110-111 David Hicks: Slim Aarons/Premium Archive/Getty Images. Interior: Fritz von der Schulenburg/The Interior Archive, designer David Hicks.

Pages 112-113 Tory: Patrick Demarchelier/Art + Commerce. Family photo: Barbara Vaughn.

Page 114 Column 1: Fragrance bottle: Ilan Rubin/Trunk Archive. Model: Jennifer Livingston/Trunk Archive. Column 2: Resort 2013: Norman Jean Roy/Trunk Archive; stylist: Brian Molloy/Tim Howard Management; model: Liu Wen/The Society Management. Column 4: Leonard & Evelyn Lauder at The Persian Room. Column 5: Model: Jennifer Livingston/Trunk Archive. Backstage: Jennifer Livingston/Trunk Archive; model: Katya Riabinkina/Women Management.

Page 116 Henri Matisse, *Anemones and Chinese Vase*, 1922, oil on canvas, 24 x 36.5 in. (61 x 92.7 cm); The Baltimore Museum of Art: The Cone Collection, formed by Dr. Claribel Cone and Miss Etta Cone of Baltimore, Maryland, BMA 1950.248. Photo: Mitro Hood; © 2014 Succession H. Matisse/Artists Rights Society (ARS), New York.

Page 117 Angelo Pennetta/Trunk Archive; stylist: Ethel Park; models: Laura Kampman/New York Model Management & Mirte Maas/Women Management.

Page 118 *A la poursuite des mots*: Courtesy of Bourrelier Éducation; bourrelier-education.fr. *Lolita*: Jennifer Heuer. *The Secret Garden* cover: © Jillian Tamaki, courtesy of Penguin Books. *Praia Mar*: Bernardo Carvalho © 2011, Planeta Tangerina.

Page 119 Willem de Kooning, *Marilyn Monroe*, 1954; Collection of R. R. Neuberger, New York, U.S.A./The Bridgeman Art Library © 2014 The Willem de Kooning Foundation/Artists Rights Society (ARS), New York.

Page 122 *Praise, from the Rubber Stamp Portfolio*, 1976, published 1977. One from a portfolio of 13 rubber stamps, composition (irreg): 8.0625 x 8.3125 in. (20.5 x 21.1 cm); sheet: 11 x 11 in. (28 x 28 cm). Gift of Parasol Press, Ltd. and the Publications Department of the Museum of Modern Art. The Museum of Modern Art, New York, NY, U.S.A. © 2014 Agnes Martin/Artists Rights Society (ARS), New York. Digital Image © The Museum of Modern Art/Licensed by SCALA/Art Resource, NY.

Page 123 Model: Katya Riabinkina/Women Management.

Page 129 Today: *The Inquirer Magazine* used with permission of Philadelphia Inquirer; copyright © 2014. All rights reserved.

Page 130 Gunnar Larsen/Rex Features; courtesy of Everett Collection.

Page 131 *3 Poppies, Arab Chief*, New York, 1969. Photograph by Irving Penn. Copyright © Condé Nast.

Page 132 Gordon Hull/Tory Burch LLC.

Page 133 Dan & Corina Lecca; stylist: Tabitha Simmons/Streeters; model: Ava Smith/Wilhelmina NY.

Page 134 Stylist: Brian Molloy/Tim Howard Management; model: Ruby Aldridge/Next Model Management.

Page 135 Dan & Corina Lecca; stylist: Tabitha Simmons/Streeters; models: Krystal Glynn/DNA Model Management; Antonia Wesseloh, Daria Strokous, Fei Fei Sun, Ginta Lapina, Jourdan Dunn, Valerija Sestic/Women Management; Karolina Waz/One Management; Kate King & Kinga Rajazak/IMG Models; Arizona Muse/Next Model Management; Anais Pouliot/The Society Management; Julia Dunstall/Marilyn.

Page 136 Clockwise from top left: Alma Woodsey Thomas (1891–1978), *Antares*, 1972, acrylic on canvas, 65.75 x 56.5 in. (167 x 143.5 cm). Smithsonian American Art Museum, Washington, DC, U.S.A. Photograph: Smithsonian American Art Museum, Washington DC/Art Resource, NY. Thelma Golden: Timothy Greenfield-Sanders, courtesy of The Studio Museum in Harlem. Jeanne Greenberg Rohatyn: Tom Munro/Management + Artists. Laurie Simmons, *The Love Doll: Day 31 (Geisha)*, 2011/ Image courtesy of the artist and Salon 94.

Page 138 Elgort/*Vogue*; © Condé Nast.

Page 139 Ben Vautier, *L'essential est que je communique*, 1970. Tamu McPherson: Annina Piana.

Page 140 From left, top row: The Mortimers: Mary Hilliard. Second row: the Allbrittons: Tony Powell/tony-powell.com. Third row: the Camutos: Joe Schildhorn/BFAnyc.com; Boardman, Blasberg, Wang and Santo Domingo: Joe Schildorn/BFAnyc.com. Fourth row: Mishaan: Brooke Wall. All other photos courtesy of the subjects.

Page 141 Mimi Ritzen Crawford.

Page 142 *It Gives Me Great Pleasure* by Cecil Beaton; ©1955, Weidenfeld & Nicolson/Courtesy of The Orion Publishing Group, London.

Page 144 Hawaii: © Noa Griffel, 2013. Tokyo: Gordon Hull/Tory Burch LLC.

Page 145 Top right, middle right and bottom: Vance Jacobs.

Page 150 Elgort/*Vogue*; © Condé Nast.

Page 151 Milton Avery, *Interlude*, 1960, The Philadelphia Museum of Art © 2014 Milton Avery Trust/Artists Rights Society (ARS) New York.

Pages 152-153 Recipe: Dana Minuta. *Brigitte Bardot Relaxes* © James Andanson/ Sygma/Corbis.

Page 154 Gerhard Richter, *Abstract Painting 812*, 1994 © Gerhard Richter, 2014/Marian Goodman Gallery, New York, Paris.

Page 155 Nicole Robinson: © Noa Griffel, 2013.

Pages 156-157 Models: Zuzanna Bijoch/ Next Model Management; Bette Franke, Kati Nescher/DNA Model Management; Ava Smith/Wilhelmina NY; Nadja Bender/New York Model Management; Jac Jacaziak/IMG Models; Ginta Lapina/Women Management.

Page 158 *The Cocktail Party* by T.S. Eliot (Orlando: Harcourt, 1950). Used by permission of Houghton Mifflin Harcourt Publishing Company. All rights reserved. *The Great Gatsby* cover: Aled Lewis. Ernest Hemingway cover reprinted with the permission of Scribner Publishing Group, a division of Simon & Schuster, Inc. from *The Sun Also Rises* by Ernest Hemingway; copyright © (New York, 1970); all rights reserved. Cover from *Mrs. Dalloway* by Virginia Woolf, published by The Hogarth Press, reprinted by permission of The Random House Group Limited.

Page 159 David Bailey/*Vogue*; © Condé Nast.

Pages 160-161 From left, top row: Collins: © patrickmcmullan.com; the tennis group: Marion Curtis/StarPix; Foley: David X. Prutting/BFAnyc.com; Brigette, Paolo and Robert: Mimi Ritzen Crawford. Second row: Smith: Joe Schildhorn/BFAnyc.com. Third row, inset: Wasserstein: Donna Newman; Zucker: © patrickmcmullan.com. All other photos courtesy of the subjects.

Page 163 Cover from *The Little Prince* by Antoine de Saint-Exupéry. Copyright 1943 by Houghton Mifflin Harcourt Publishing Company. Copyright © renewed 1971 by Consuelo de Saint-Exupéry; used by permission of Houghton Mifflin Harcourt Publishing Company. All rights reserved.

Pages 164-165 Gordon Hull/Tory Burch LLC. Star fruit: © Noa Griffel, 2013.

Pages 166-167 Lotusland: © Bill Dewey.

Pages 174-175 Tory: Gordon Hull/Tory Burch LLC.

Pages 178-179 Clockwise from top left: Le Petit Trianon: Janelle McCulloch. Romy Schneider on the set of Jacques Deray's film *La Piscine*/Gamma-Keystone/ Getty Images. Spring 2014: Angelo Pennetta/Trunk Archive; stylist: Ethel Park; model: Caroline Brasch Nielsen/The Society Management. Elgort/*Vogue Living*; © Condé Nast. Horst/ *Vogue*; © Condé Nast. Spring 2014: Angelo Pennetta/Trunk Archive; stylist: Ethel Park; models: Lindsey Wixson/ The Society Management; Bette Franke/ DNA Model Management.

Page 180 Bjorn Iooss.

Page 181 Interiors: John Spinks. Top: Sheep by Les Lalanne, *Mouton de laine*, 1965/ Courtesy Paul Kasmin Gallery; sculpture over door by Lynda Benglis, *Gold Luster*, 1981/ Courtesy Cheim & Read, New York/ © Lynda Benglis/ Licensed by VAGA New York, NY. Bottom, from left: Anh Duong, *Lady Q*, 2006; *Untitled* © Hans-Peter Feldmann, courtesy 303 Gallery, New York; Allison Edge, *Ray*, 2006.

Pages 182-183 Norman Jean Roy/ Trunk Archive.

Page 186 Gordon Hull/Tory Burch LLC.

Pages 188-189 *The Philadelphia Inquirer* used with permission of Philadelphia Inquirer; copyright © 2014. All rights reserved.

Page 192 Gordon Hull/Tory Burch LLC.

Page 194 Tory & Nick: © Noa Griffel, 2013.

Page 195 Tory & stepdaughters: Barbara Vaughn. The boys: Norman Jean Roy/Trunk Archive, originally for *Vogue*.

Page 196 nando ponce.

Page 197 Demarchelier/*W*; © Condé Nast.

Pages 198-199 François Halard/Trunk Archive, originally for *Vogue*.

Pages 200-201 Clockwise from top left: Cecil Beaton courtesy of Condé Nast. Tory: Matteo Prandoni/BFAnyc.com. *Andy Warhol & Edie Sedgwick*, New York, 1964; photo: Ugo Mulas © Ugo Mulas Heirs; all rights reserved. Warhol: © 2014 The Andy Warhol Foundation for the Visual Arts, Inc. / Artists Rights Society (ARS), New York. *Les pains de Picasso*, 1952 © Robert Doisneau/Gamma Rapho, Picasso; © 2014 Estate of Pablo Picasso / Artists Rights Society (ARS), New York. Stephen Sumner, *White Noise*, 2013. Jasper Johns, *Jubilee*, 1959, oil and collage on canvas; art © Jasper Johns/Licensed by VAGA New York; photograph by Jamie Stukenberg. Louise Bourgeois, *Maman*, 1999; art © The Easton Foundation/Licensed by VAGA New York, NY; photo: © Nathan Strange/AP/Corbis.

Pages 202-203 Norman Jean Roy/Trunk Archive; stylist: Ethel Park; models: Caroline Brasch Nielsen/The Society Management, Tilda Lindstam/IMG Models. Porcelain: © Jean Paul Gourdon/Galerie Démesure, L'Isle-sur-la-Sorgue; photo: Dan Palmer.

Pages 204-205 From left, top row: Fiona Kotur: William Furniss; Winfrey: © Harpo Studios, Inc.; photographer: George Burns; Wyatt: © Phoebe Rourke-Ghabriel. Second row: Hernandez, McCollough and Rodriguez: Rabbani & Solimene Photography. Third row: Tisch: Julie Skarratt Photography; D'Souza Wolfe: Jennifer Livingston/Trunk Archive. Fourth row: Gregory: © patrickmcmullan.com; Mota and Rockefeller: Neil Rasmus/ BFAnyc.com; Mortimer, Lindemann and Ganek: Mimi Ritzen Crawford; Lauder: Simon Upton. All other photos courtesy of the subjects.

Page 212 Tom Wesselmann, *Study for Great American Nude #68*, 1966, art © Estate of Tom Wesselmann/Licensed by VAGA, New York, NY.

Page 214 François Halard/Trunk Archive, originally for *Vogue*. Artwork: Walton Ford, *So Panteth My Soul After Thee*, 2001, watercolor, gouache, ink and pencil on paper. Artwork courtesy of the artist and Paul Kasmin Gallery.

Page 215 Walton Ford, *Algiers Point*, 2013. Artwork courtesy of the artist and Paul Kasmin Gallery.

Pages 216-217 Julia Hetta/*T Magazine*.

Page 221 Norman Jean Roy/Trunk Archive; stylist: Brian Molloy/Tim Howard Management; models: Tati Cotlar/Next Model Management, Ophelie Rupp/ DNA Model Management.

Page 225 © Christophe Boisvieux/Corbis.

Page 226 Gordon Hull/Tory Burch LLC.

Page 227 "Nothing Gold Can Stay" from the book *The Poetry of Robert Frost*, edited by Edward Connery Lathem. Copyright © 1923, 1969 by Henry Holt and Company, LLC. Copyright © 1951 by Robert Frost. Used by permission of Henry Holt and Company, LLC. All rights reserved.

Pages 228-229 Francesca DiMattio, *Orgy Pot*, 2012/Courtesy of the artist and Salon 94. Yves Klein, *Gold Table*, Plexiglas, glass, gold leaf, stainless-steel feet, 100 x 125 x 36.5 cm © 2014 Yves Klein /Artists Rights Society (ARS), New York/ ADAGP, Paris.

Page 230 Mimi Ritzen Crawford.

Page 233 Runway: Dan & Corina Lecca; stylist: Samira Nasr/Management + Artists; model: Tabea Koebach/IMG Models.

Page 235 Jonny Valiant.

Pages 236-237 Clockwise from top left: Jean-Michel Basquiat, *All Colored Cast (Part II)*, 1982 © The Estate of Jean-Michel Basquiat/ADAGP, Paris/ARS, New York 2014; acrylic and pencil and collage on wood support, 152.5x152.5 cm, private collection; photo: Banque d'Images, ADAGP/Art Resource, NY. Yves Klein, *Gold Table* (see pages 228-229 above); Gustav Klimt (1862–1918): *Portrait of Adele Bloch-Bauer I*, 1907; oil, silver and gold on canvas; this acquisition made available in part through the generosity of the heirs of The Estate of Ferdinand and Adele Bloch-Bauer; photo: John Gilliand, Neue Galerie New York/Art Resource, NY. Britt Ekland by Slim Aarons/Premium Collection/ Getty Images. Andy Warhol, *A Gold Book*, 1957; image and artwork © 2014 The Andy Warhol Foundation for the Visual Arts, Inc./ Artists Rights Society (ARS), New York.

Page 239 Donald Judd, *Untitled*, 1969; copper, ten units with 9-inch intervals; 9 x 40 x 31 in. (22.9 x 101.6 x 78.7 cm) each; 180x40x31 in. (457.2 x 101.6 x 78.7 cm) overall. Panza Collection, 1991. The Solomon R. Guggenheim Foundation. Art © Judd Foundation. Licensed by VAGA, New York, NY. Photo: The Solomon R. Guggenheim Foundation/Art Resource, NY.

Page 240 Jennifer Livingston/Trunk Archive; model: Ava Smith/Wilhelmina NY.

Page 241 Irving Penn, *Ginkgo Leaves*, New York, 1990; copyright © by The Irving Penn Foundation.

Page 242 Jonny Valiant.

Page 243 Norman Jean Roy/Trunk Archive; stylist: Brian Molloy/Tim Howard Management; model: Ophelie Rupp/DNA Model Management.

Page 244 Paint laboratory, Porzellan Manufaktur Nymphenburg.

Page 245 Douglas Friedman/ Trunk Archive.

Page 246 Illustration: De La Vega and Tory Burch.

Page 250 Carmen Almon courtesy of The Chinese Porcelain Company.

Page 251 Neil Rasmus/BFAnyc.com.

Pages 254-255 Pookie Burch.

Photos by Noa Griffel: **pages 16, 20, 21, 24-27, 32-34, 36-37, 39, 42-43, 46-47, 53, 55, 58, 61, 62, 68-69, 70, 72-73, 74-75, 80-81, 90-91, 94-97, 100, 103, 109, 112-115, 120-121, 123, 126, 139, 142, 152, 156-157, 158, 160-161, 163, 168, 170, 172-174, 176-177, 178-179, 184-185, 188-191, 193, 204-205, 210-212, 220, 222-224, 228-229, 233, 236-237, 244, 246, 248-249, 250.**

Back Cover
Photograph by Patrick Demarchelier/ Art + Commerce.

Photographs by Pookie Burch. Rome, 2010

TORY BURCH

CREATIVE DIRECTOR: HONOR BRODIE
DIRECTOR OF EDITORIAL: NANDINI D'SOUZA WOLFE
DESIGN DIRECTOR: LOUISA GENT
SENIOR PHOTO EDITOR: ALLY LEWIS
DIRECTOR OF CREATIVE OPERATIONS: SASHA TULCHIN

BOOK AND COVER DESIGN: EMILY WARDWELL

ABRAMS EDITOR: REBECCA KAPLAN
ABRAMS PRODUCTION MANAGER: ANET SIRNA-BRUDER

COVER ART:
BEAUTIFUL PRIMAL URGES RUG
100% WOOL, 130 KNOTS PER SQUARE INCH, HANDWOVEN
3000 MM (DIAMETER)
© DAMIEN HIRST AND SCIENCE LTD. ALL RIGHTS RESERVED / DACS, LONDON / ARS, NY 2014
COURTESY OF OTHER CRITERIA.

BACK COVER:
PHOTOGRAPH BY PATRICK DEMARCHELIER/ART + COMMERCE

LIBRARY OF CONGRESS CONTROL NUMBER: 2013945691

ISBN: 978-1-4197-0747-6

ABRAMS BOOKS ARE AVAILABLE AT SPECIAL DISCOUNTS WHEN PURCHASED IN QUANTITY
FOR PREMIUMS AND PROMOTIONS AS WELL AS FUNDRAISING OR EDUCATIONAL USE.
SPECIAL EDITIONS CAN ALSO BE CREATED TO SPECIFICATION. FOR DETAILS, CONTACT
SPECIALSALES@ABRAMSBOOKS.COM OR THE ADDRESS BELOW.

ABRAMS
THE ART OF BOOKS SINCE 1949
115 WEST 18TH STREET
NEW YORK, NY 10011
WWW.ABRAMSBOOKS.COM